Preparing to Be Next in Line

A Guide to the Principalship

Kevin A. Gorman

ROWMAN & LITTLEFIELD EDUCATION
A division of
ROWMAN & LITTLEFIELD PUBLISHERS, INC.
Lanham • New York • Toronto • Plymouth, UK

Published by Rowman & Littlefield Education
A division of Rowman & Littlefield Publishers, Inc.
A wholly owned subsidiary of The Rowman & Littlefield Publishing Group, Inc.
4501 Forbes Boulevard, Suite 200, Lanham, Maryland 20706
http://www.rowmaneducation.com

Estover Road, Plymouth PL6 7PY, United Kingdom

British Library Cataloguing in Publication Information Available

Library of Congress Cataloging-in-Publication Data

Gorman, Kevin, 1953-
Preparing to be next in line : a guide to the principalship / Kevin Gorman.
p. cm.
Includes bibliographical references and index.
ISBN 978-1-61048-628-6 (cloth : alk. paper) -- ISBN 978-1-61048-629-3 (pbk. : alk. paper) -- ISBN
978-1-61048-630-9 (electronic)
1. School principals--Professional relationships. 2. Educational leadership. I. Title.
LB2831.9.G67 2012
371.2'012--dc23

2011050437

Printed in the United States of America

"Leadership by example sustains trust."

—Robert K. Greenleaf, *Servant Leadership* (1977)

Contents

Foreword

How many times have you read an article or a book on educational leadership or best practices in the field of education and wondered, "Is this author really any good?" or "Does this person *really* walk the talk?" Let's face it, as practitioners we look at many articles and books with a skeptical eye. It is one thing to write about being in "the game" from the sidelines as many educational theorists do, and it is another to write from the perspective of being one of the players in the game, as Dr. Gorman does.

Dr. Kevin Gorman asked the two of us, his prior boss and his current boss, to write this foreword. That takes guts. We know how Dr. Gorman operates. We have seen him at his best and worst. Knowing what we know about Dr. Gorman, we can't think of a more qualified person to write this book. He brings the latest educational theories, matches them to real-life experiences, and offers new and aspiring building leaders practical advice essential to their success. Too often the academic texts available to aspiring and practicing school leaders miss practical application, which is such an important component. This book includes a strong focus on practical application.

As an author, Dr. Gorman writes from a vantage point of one who has done it all. He has been a classroom teacher, coach, special-needs teacher and supervisor, principal, college professor, and executive director of pupil services. Dr. Gorman has had the opportunity to observe new principals and building leaders from a variety of perspectives. His readers will benefit from the unique vantage point from which he writes.

So with regard to the questions posed earlier—"Is this author really any good?" and "Does this person *really* walk the talk?"—we feel that we are best qualified to answer, when it comes to Dr. Kevin Gorman. Kevin excels at all that he does. As a high-school principal, he made teaching and learning a high priority. He focused on the needs of each student while fostering a real sense of community among staff and parents. He moved the needle academically and challenged all staff to help each student succeed.

As the executive director of pupil services, he is responsible for overseeing those services in the district that support student learning. Special education, counseling, OT, PT, student registration, and school psychology are just some of the areas for which he is responsible. His perspective is most valuable, as it is not from the top position, as with a superintendent, but rather from that of a trusted colleague and fellow participant in the game. He has the advantage of having the view from the trenches and the war room, and this perspective makes all the difference to the reader.

Kevin Gorman is relentless as he advocates for his students, staff, and programs. He handles the most complicated issues and always seems to make the right call. He may upset staff, administrators, parents, and state officials from time to time, but his blunt yet fair nature gives him the courage to say what others wish they could. He is loyal and trusted, yet he does not always do what we want him to do, and this is fine with us.

Kevin Gorman is the kind of leader that we need in education today—one who cares deeply for students and staff, wants to help every student reach his or her greatest potential, and has the courage to say what needs to be said. We can't think of a more committed, caring, and compassionate leader to help the next generation of school leaders develop the courage to make the tough calls and the charisma to get others to follow.

We know that this book will be a key resource for you, now and in the future.

Brad Rieger, PhD, Superintendent
Thomas L. Hosler, Superintendent

Preface

So now you have been hired as a new principal, and have approximately three weeks to ready the building for the staff and students. Where do you begin?

What kind of leader do you want to be? What types of relationships with staff, students, and parents do you want to establish? How do you propose to effectively communicate with everyone? What is your building budget? Who is responsible for keeping the books and submitting the purchase orders? Is the building clean and ready for opening day? Have you read the teacher contract? Who are the teacher and student leaders in the building? What impact do the head custodian and secretary have on your success? How do you contact the leader of the parent group?

These are all very short questions with very complicated answers. There is no right or wrong way to open a school or lead a building. However, it is imperative that you start out in a positive manner, as first impressions can create a great beginning, or provide a gap between you and staff members from the inception.

This book is just a "how to" guide for beginning as a new building professional, and getting started in a positive manner with teachers, classified-staff members, students, parents, and the community at large. Today, everything in education must be evidence based before it can be considered best practice. This text is your guide in integrating research into professional practice, with a section in each chapter stating the current research as it applies to that chapter. In most texts the research is integrated into the narrative, and the reader must locate and highlight the theory with the evidence-based research or practice. This guide is different and novel, in that the research is summarized at the beginning of each chapter, separately from and prior to the integration of that research into practice. Therefore, you can pick and choose your question, and find the research later if you so desire.

This guide may be read in its entirety, or utilized as suggested answers to specific questions that you may have acquired on your first few days. This guide will not answer all of your questions, as every district is different, but it should provide you with enough information to get you started thinking about what type of leader you want to be, and how to get started on the road to becoming a successful leader.

Chapter One

Where Do I Begin?

THEORY

Effective leadership occurs when a building leader can determine the developmental level and needs of a building, looking particularly at the classified and the certified staff members. One method the principal can utilize is developing questionnaires to determine the needs of the building and the employees; another is personally asking the employees questions. This type of principal is utilizing *situational leadership*. The survey will indicate if the building staff does better with a highly directive leader with low emotional support or a highly directive and highly supportive role in leadership.

Some employees need high support and very low directives, and still others need low support and low directives (Blanchard 1985). Situational leadership does not give a leader all of the answers in terms of motivating employees to different levels of support or direction.

Another form of leading is *transformational leadership*, which is very popular today in the school literature. A leader sets a goal with his or her stakeholders and assists in working with and facilitating the accomplishment of that goal. Strong organizations reinvent themselves to utilize practices that have been proved to be effective (Fullan 2008, 77). One of the main reasons this is so popular is that it is goal and data driven by the team. The difficulty in this style of leadership is that the leader must be inspiring in order to develop a trust factor with the stakeholders and achieve the goal.

In some cases it is easier to direct a staff than engage a staff, but engaging a group of educators will produce a better outcome than ordering a group of educators to accomplish the same task (Downton 1973). MetLife conducted a survey of the American teacher and found that 93 percent of the time, teachers work in isolation from other teachers (including time spent after school in planning and grading). Teachers are disconnected from one another, and their professional development is extremely fragmented and not connected to their classroom work (Carroll and Doerr 2010).

Data is the backbone of decision making in schools. Areas of data to consider are the school and district report cards, which break down the attendance, test scores, annual yearly progress, and truancy and graduation rates. This is something that hopefully was usually utilized prior to the interview for the position that has just been attained. Schoolwide data also needs to be analyzed by having teachers review subject objectives and student performance and determine if the target goals are clear and measurable, and if interventions are in place for those students who are struggling (Rourke and Hartzman 2008).

Other factors to consider prior to setting goals are the schedule, and the opportunity for students to learn with staff. The use of time is critical in teaching adolescents, along with monitoring what is going on in the classroom and ensuring students achieve and are successful.

Parental involvement and school climate also play an essential role in setting realistic goals. The administrative leadership of the building, and the teacher leaders working and cooperating together on the behalf of students, should all be considered in goal setting for the first year (Marzano 2003).

Another form of leading is *trait leadership*, which has been examined for years. Traits that individuals might hope to achieve, and that leaders are perceived as having, include intelligence, self-confidence, determination, integrity, and sociability (Northhouse 2010). Most of these traits are easy to understand; however, sociability is a more qualitative trait that is difficult to measure. Leaders who display *sociability* are friendly, outgoing, and tactful, and sensitive to people's needs, and they demonstrate an honest concern for the well-being of stakeholders.

INTEGRATING THEORY INTO PRACTICE

The principal's first encounters are usually with the custodian and the secretary. Though they may have been a part of the interview committee, the new principal has no idea what their relationships with the previous principal were like, and what their current fears and concerns might be with respect to having a new employer. As a new principal, it is imperative to develop a pleasant working relationship with both the secretary and the custodian. The secretary can make or break a new administrator, as he or she is the first voice or first person a parent will encounter upon entering the building. The custodian also is extremely important, ensuring a safe and clean environment.

Every building has a personality that reflects the leadership style of the principal. If a building is not clean, or if a secretary ignores a parent or is rude to a parent in person or on the phone, this will be a direct reflection on the principal, and can cause issues from day one. Customer service and high expectations are extremely important, and these begin with the building leader.

Initially, an informal meeting is a good way to get to know the secretary and the head custodian. This can be done with the two of them together or separately, depending upon the choice of the leader. Even though it is informal, having an agenda (not necessarily shared in advance) will keep the meeting moving along, as well as communicating your organizational style and record-keeping ability. Simple things such as discussing the type of communication system you desire and reflecting upon what was done prior to your arriving will be good ways to glean initial information.

Discussing the plan for preparing the building for opening day is essential, as the school will open, and students will come whether it is ready or not ready. Most schools have a cleaning schedule or a plan to ensure that the school is ready. A principal should ask for a copy of that cleaning schedule, along with any mailings that were sent out to parents or any copies of items or information that need to be mailed to parents. Inquire about the leadership of the parent booster group(s), as well as upper-class student leaders. Ask for telephone numbers so that you can begin to establish communication and connections with your customers and stakeholders.

Explain how, as the principal, you would like to have the office function. Who is responsible for the budget, and the purchase-order system? Ensure that you have a good understanding of this system, and of who besides you is responsible for monitoring this budget.

A follow-up meeting with the treasurer is a great way to ensure that what was shared with you by the office staff is how the district and the board of education want the financial system integrated into the system. If this is your first position, then ask for clarification of past organizational styles that the secretary has utilized. Ask the secretary what he or she would like to see stay the same, and what he or she would like to see changed. Ask why he or she sees this style of organization as necessary for the operation of the office and the school, and the betterment of communication within and without the office setting. Explain what you need from the secretary, including confidentiality, student-records accessibility, telephone etiquette, and stopping computer work to greet parents or students entering the building. This will set the tone for a user-friendly office.

Ask the custodian for a tour of the building, noting general concerns, maintenance issues, supply concerns, and the custodial-staff chain of command. As you tour the building, make note of problem areas that could be security risks, and/or how the cleaned rooms, lockers, or hallways reflect what you think they should look like after being cleaned. Attention to detail will ensure a clean and safe building. It is also a reflection of your leadership style.

The next meetings that should be scheduled should include the cafeteria coordinator in your building. The cafeteria will be a hot spot for safety concerns if it is not monitored properly. Again, have an agenda that will drive your questions on how the food service flows in this building, and who in the past has monitored the students.

Contact the parent group leaders for your building. This might include the PTA officers, the band- and athletic-booster leaders, and leaders for any other clubs or co-curriculars that exist in your building. It might be beneficial, depending upon the timeline, to meet in a large group and establish a regular meeting schedule. Again, an agenda would facilitate the meeting's moving along, and you gather the information you need to understand past concerns and current needs.

Ask what is working and what is not working in the building. You will receive a broad amount of responses with varied concerns. Pay attention to common themes. If, for example, transportation continuously emerges as a concern, you can build tremendous support by addressing this issue early. In very active schools, these leaders will have their own agendas to combine with your agenda as the principal.

Teacher leaders are next on the agenda. Invite the leaders or department heads to a meeting. Sometimes an informal get-together with food will reveal your leadership style to teachers, as well as give you an idea of some of the communication concerns that might be present within the staff culture of the building. If you purchase some snacks and lemonade, teachers will be more relaxed and willing to share. Lead the meeting by having a chart that declares what the teachers would like to keep that has been working well, what they would like to change or stop, and what suggestions they have for creating an even better situation for the betterment of the students and staff morale.

Having this type of informal meeting, and ensuring that all the department heads or individual stakeholders who are the unofficial leaders within the building from the teaching and counseling staff are present, will reveal a great amount of information to you as to what the teaching culture is like in the building and what areas need your attention. The chart will allow you to see what the staff leaders see as a priority, and will also assist you in determining possible future problems and possible goals to work on together. This give and take of feedback will allow the staff to see you as a good listener, which is essential to leading a successful building.

Too often, principals like to talk. In this situation, ask probing questions, but just listen to unearth the concerns and problems that have possibly caused the school to not be as successful as it could be; or maybe you'll find that the staff thinks the school is great and does not need any changes. Going from good to great is usually a more difficult transition because staffs do not see the need for change. Thank this group of people, and assure them that you will communicate regularly with them, and that you will return to their concerns, as a building staff, at a later date. Make sure that whatever you commit to doing, in terms of meeting or giving feedback, you follow through. This directly ties in to your integrity, which is a proved leadership trait for successful principals.

Your next meeting needs to be with the student leaders. This could include class officers, presidents of clubs, or team captains. Make sure you have snacks for this meeting, and follow the same format that you used with the staff members. This will give you some comparisons as to the critical issues within the building. Take this information home and study it to determine the problems that exist across all areas, and the things that seem to be working well for everyone. It is very difficult to make broad changes the first year in a building.

The first year, an administrator tends to listen and take information in as it affects his or her leadership; the second year, the administrator breaks even; and the third year, the leader gives back and can make the essential changes, based upon data, to ensure a successful, safe building with a healthy school culture. Many new administrators feel pressure to make their mark by changing something during the first year of service. To make sweeping changes or even small changes without realizing how sacred the affected items may be to staff can be the undoing of a new administrator.

Make an appointment with the superintendent or your immediate supervisor to determine what his or her concerns are about the building, and compare that information to all of the other perspectives you have received. You now should have the beginnings of an understanding of what you are walking into as a new leader—and what appear to be the needs of the constituents, as you compare this information to the written mission and goals already established in the building.

With this information, begin to plan with teacher leadership and your assistants, if you have any, opening day for staff, and opening day for students. Planning for the start of school is the beginning work that must be accomplished before opening day for staff and opening day for students.

CASE STUDIES

- As you leave your new office after your initial visit to the building, long before your official contract begins, you meet in the hallway a teacher who is the building union representative, who will be part of your staff. You greet him and introduce yourself to him as the new principal. He shares with you that the staff really did not want you as the principal, but rather another local candidate whom the entire staff liked and respected. *What do you do, and what is your response?*

- When you go in to meet the veteran assistant principal who will be working for you this school year, he or she appears angry, and does not acknowledge your presence. You reintroduce yourself, though you know you met him or her when you toured the school as a potential candidate. Blindly you ask what seems to be wrong, and are abruptly told he or she interviewed for the job and you now have the position. *What do you say or do to ensure that your working relationship is effective?*

- As you tour the building on your first contracted day as principal, you notice that summer cleaning has not been completed in one hallway. There are student desks and file cabinets in the hallway. It is so crowded you cannot get through to the end of the hall. There appears to be no one around, so you go back and ask your secretary to page the custodians. She shares with you that they are all on vacation, for the next two weeks. School starts in ten days. The previous principal approved the vacation time last May. *What is your next step?*

CHAPTER REFLECTIONS

- Beginning as a new building leader can be grueling the first few weeks on the job. Determining the type of leader you want to be as a secondary principal is difficult to imagine without meeting all of the players in and out of your building. You have read the literature on great theories of leadership, which sound wonderful on paper; however, the difficulty arises when you have to apply these theories to your building and your stakeholders.

- The first few weeks should be spent getting an understanding of the current status of readiness for opening in the fall. You need to attempt to meet as many people as possible, and develop your own system for remembering names and positions.

- Reviewing the local and building report cards will give you an introduction into some of the building data. It will not tell you how or why the scores are what they are on the scorecard, but it will give you a sense of where you need to be as a building.

- Understanding what transpired before you came is a great way to figure out where the building is currently. Develop questions for each group you meet with, and note the variations. The assistant principal, athletic director, secretary, and custodian can give you an understanding of the mechanics of the building, and the operation in general.

- Taking this data and comparing it to other information you can attempt to gather from other department chairs or unofficial leaders should give you a true picture of some of the operational and building and personnel-training needs.
- Remember, you cannot do it all in one day, and it can be very overwhelming at first. Good luck!

REFERENCES

Blanchard, K. 1985. *SLII: A Situational Approach to Managing People*. Escondido, CA: Blanchard Training and Development.

Carroll, T., and H. Doerr. 2010. "Learning Teams and the Future of Learning." *Education Week* 39, no. 39.

Downton, J. V. 1973. *Rebel Leadership: Commitment and Charisma in a Revolutionary Process*. New York: Free Press.

Fullan, M. 2008. *The Six Secrets of Change: What the Best Leaders Do to Help Their Organizations Survive and Thrive*. San Francisco: Jossey-Bass.

Marzano, R. J. 2003. *What Works in Schools: Translating Research into Action*. Alexandria, VA: ASCD.

Northhouse, P. G. 2010. *Leadership Theory and Practice*. 5th ed. Thousand Oaks, CA: Sage.

Rourke, J., and M. Hartzman. 2009. "Theodore High School: Positive Attitudes." *Principal Leadership* 9, no. 10, 40–43.

Chapter Two

Goal Setting

THEORY

Setting measurable goals is the keystone for a principal to establish high expectations with a clear articulate vision that promotes high standards and reflects a commitment to excellent school practice. Goals need to be clear, concise, and measurable. The goals need to be based upon the needs of the particular organization, and they should reflect an action-plan delivery system that sets a timeline for completion or review, obstacles to overcome, and action steps or objectives to accomplish the components of the goal(s) (Hersey, Blanchard, and Johnson 1996). Continuous review and evaluation of these goals is critical to ensure there are specific learning targets.

Action plans prioritize the sequence of events that need to occur to accomplish and complete a goal, determine who is to be responsible for each portion of the sequence, and determine the timeline within which a measurable result with a defined outcome will be accomplished. All goals should have a revision component to ensure that if the goal is not mastered, the feedback indicated will allow for the reasons for nonsuccess, and a clear path will be laid for redirection and action steps to attain the original desired outcome or the envisioned new outcome (Hersey, Blanchard, and Johnson 1996).

Goals cannot be developed in isolation. The leader needs to determine the group readiness level in developing and implementing the different stages of the goal development. If the team has not realized the urgency of developing goals, the implementation of the action plan will be difficult or impossible (Hersey, Blanchard, and Johnson 1996). Most plans of principals are unsuccessful because the principal has not considered how the larger culture or local building norms will react to innovations or strategies undertaken without the building's or community's input or suggestions (Senge et al. 1999).

Too often the administrator has not established a trust factor with the staff because of being new to the position or the district. Change requires leadership over a long period of time (Goldberg 2000). That time period will vary depending upon past administrative tenures within the given building. The staff needs to feel a sense of urgency to buy into or own a goal, as well as achieving some small wins or goal accomplishments in the process (Fullan 2008). The initial goals should be small and achievable to assist the momentum of the faculty and stakeholders in the initial weeks of implementation within the school (Reeves 2009).

Remaining consistent is the other essential requirement for finding success in goal achievement. Too often the latest in-service training has nothing to do with the established goals, and that new initiative clouds the effectiveness of the established goals that were developed from the beginning of the school year. It is imperative that the principal establish only a few goals so that he or she can maintain focus and monitor and collect data on the goals that were established from the beginning (White 2009).

Self-assessment is essential in being an instructional leader. Too often the principal loses his or her way managing building issues instead of attempting to be the instructional leader, guiding, empowering, and anchoring the new approach or goals into the existing culture (Kotter 2006). It is imperative that the management of the building issues does not override the time that is needed to be an instructional leader.

INTEGRATING THEORY INTO PRACTICE

Staff buy-in is the most difficult task a new principal must sell. The staff need to know with whom they are working as a building leader, and what is in it for them. In the previous chapter, information was gathered from many stakeholders regarding strengths, weaknesses and concerns. It is essential that the staff get to know who the new leader is, and whether he or she walks the talk and models the values that the newly suggested needs and goals illustrate.

Utilizing the information gathered previously, along with mandated state and federal priorities, the principal should divide the staff into groups of no more than ten staff members including teachers, custodians, and secretaries, and again strategize in the groups regarding the strengths, weaknesses, and achievements of the staff and of the school. Ensure that departments are broken apart to get a more accurate representation of the concerns. This then can be put on posters and hung in the lounge after the information has been shared with everyone on staff. It is a starting point. You may want to use some of the information that you gleaned from your initial meetings with teacher and counselor leaders as a springboard for starting discussions. This also reinforces to those people that you heard them at your initial meetings and that you took their ideas and concerns seriously.

As the leader, it is imperative that you check how those weaknesses and strengths match the previous information acquired by the other stakeholders before school began. A strong indicator of the readiness of the staff to take a serious look at their progress and goal-setting abilities will be how well the principal matches the concerns and strengths to the previously acquired information. The staff must feel a sense of empowerment and urgency to establish new goals and not settle for complacency.

The leader must be a type of cheerleader and facilitator to create the need for change. The leader can use some of the people he or she initially met with before school began to help the cause within the departments. There will always be a few negative comments or intentional sabotage, but for a leader the needs and the goals need to come first, and there is never 100 percent buy-in from a staff. If 100 percent buy-in is requested, the school will never move forward. Once the weaknesses have been established and the district's external needs have been added, allow staff members to indicate on the posters which weaknesses interest them professionally and sign up for the items that they are willing to help improve. This does two things; it gives staff members input regarding what they see as worth fixing, and it publicly announces the new priorities.

Assemble the information in an orderly fashion and establish focus groups as the beginning of the goal-setting process. Use some of the theory as short reads for the focus groups so that they feel empowered to make critical decisions and recommendations to staff based upon the current literature. Utilizing that strategy, empowers the group to reinforce their goals or their suggested remedies for the weaknesses or problems that were presented earlier. There should be no more than about three to five goals, as any more would be difficult for you to monitor.

All staff development should be tied in to those goals, so there is one target for the year. By involving the staff in the process, you will ensure that there will be more ownership. The saboteurs who like things the way they are because they have never had a problem will be watching the leader closely to eye a mistake or a move off the target. That is why it is important to have fewer goals, so the leader can monitor the progress as it unfolds.

Distribute report cards or evaluations to staff monthly or quarterly to keep the staff focused on the goals and to keep the leader's priorities in line with what he or she committed to at the beginning of the year. This will allow the leader to walk the talk and will begin to build trust with the staff. The leader should also provide snacks to celebrate any progress or short-term wins that each goal has seen throughout the year, so the staff can feel some success and a sense of purpose for continued commitment to the goal(s).

Throughout the process, personalize things and positively and publicly reinforce the staff members who are working toward accomplishing the goal(s). This will be additional motivation to find and work for success.

CASE STUDIES

- You hold your first staff meeting, and you notice many of the teachers sit in the back of the cafeteria. The cafeteria is the only room conducive to the purpose and large enough to hold your staff, which numbers over 100 teachers. As the acoustics are poor in this room, you have to use a microphone to project, which is very impersonal. *How do you make this situation more personal and intimate?*
- Some of the staff members are grading papers or reading the sports page of the local paper while you are talking at your first staff meeting. You have tried using proximity to stop the inappropriate behavior, but to no avail. *How do you remedy this situation?*
- Opening day for staff is here at last. You have had twenty days to prepare for the opening meeting, and you are very excited to begin your journey with your staff. When the meeting is to begin, only a few staff members are in the cafeteria. When you question why no one else is present when you sent out the e-mail on the time of the meeting well in advance, you are informed that according to past practice with the former principal, opening day was always a teacher workday, and information was shared in a memo so teachers could get ready for the arrival of the students the next day. *How do you handle this situation?*

CHAPTER REFLECTIONS

- There are two types of goal setting to think about as a new principal. The first involves your personal goals for the building, and what you want the building to look like as a building culture and how clean, warm, and welcoming physically you hope the building will be for new students and families. *The other goal to think about, which is even more important, is positively impacting current practice.*
- You have collected bits and pieces of information through observations, interviews, and discussions with many of the leading members of your new staff. Somehow you need to review these scattered puzzle pieces, and

develop some form of organization for yourself as to what has happened in the past that has worked, and what has happened in the past that has not worked. Based upon your personal goals, you need to determine where you want the building to be in one year and where you want the building to be in five years.

- One way of organizing this information is to develop a survey, to get all of the stakeholders involved. Stakeholders include teachers, classified-staff members, students, and parents. This will provide you much-needed data, and should assist you in your goal-setting efforts.

REFERENCES

Fullan, M. 2008. *The Six Secrets of Change: What the Best Leaders Do to Help Their Organizations Survive and Thrive*. San Francisco: Jossey-Bass.

Goldberg, M. F. 2000. "Leadership for Change: An Interview with John Goodlad." *Phi Delta Kappan* 82, no. 1, 82–85.

Hersey, P., K. Blanchard, and D. Johnson. 1998. *Management of Organizational Behavior*. New York: Jossey-Bass.

Kotter, J. P. 2006. *Leading Change*. Boston: Harvard Business School Press.

Reeves, D. B. 2009. *Leading Change in Your School*. Alexandria, VA: ASCD.

Senge, P., A. Kleiner, C. Roberts, G. Roth, R. Ross, and B. Smith. 2009. *The Dance of Change*. New York: Doubleday.

White, S. *Leadership Maps*. 2009. Englewood, CO: Lead and Learn Press.

Chapter Three

The Assistant-Principal Role

THEORY

The assistant principal walks the walk of a true middle manager. This position is oftentimes very isolated, and characterized by interrupted, scattered, and fragmented short tasks, or issues and problems to be solved following no particular pattern or scheme (Peterson and Kelly 2001). The assistant principal usually takes the position as a stepping-stone to his or her own building.

The problem is, the job description of the assistant principal is usually very narrow and usually involves discipline or scheduling student activities, while offering little to no experience with curriculum development, common assessments, budgeting, or leadership (Bloom and Krovetz 2001). The position can become lost in clerical discipline and not touch on instructional leadership at all (Wong 2009). The assistant role should be more like an apprenticeship that leads the assistant to his or her own building by allowing the assistant to share common goals with the principal, his or her mentor (Bloom and Krovetz).

The challenge for the principal is to find and take the time to develop the skill set of the assistant so that he or she is more of a support system to the principal, while learning the ropes of the principalship. This requires preplanning, and setting up weekly meetings with an agenda that consists of discussing a common philosophy, mission, and goals—rather than impulsively coming up with quick, undocumented, inconsistent solutions to daily problems that may blow up again later due to the impulsive solutions and the lack of documentation. The two should become partners in working together for the same outcome, rather than in isolation, taking on individual tasks.

The challenge for the assistant is that of learning the principal's style of leadership, expectations, communication style, and, finally, core belief system about teachers, student learning, and leadership. Collaboration is the key as the principal and his or her assistant work together through intentional, preplanned communicative interactions (West 2011).

Great principals and their assistants model care, and through their consistent example the building culture becomes one of caring. Fear of administration does not work in establishing a healthy learning environment. Strong leadership is evident in buildings that utilize a web of healthy professional relationships, led by the principal and his or her partner or apprentice, the assistant principal (Rooney 2003).

Many times an assistant will be assigned a group of teachers to evaluate, in a separate process from the principal's evaluation of a different group of teachers. This scenario creates problems as the focus of the evaluations may not be consistent, and each administrator may be looking at different criteria, from student engagement to the examination of a particular standard. Teachers tend to not be an active part of the evaluation process, but rather listeners, after they put on their A game when they know the administrator will be in to observe (DuFour and Marzano 2009). A lack of regular communication between the principal and the assistant creates many inconsistencies in the evaluation process. This lack of communication and lack of best practice tends to create stagnation and stops a school from moving forward.

The assistant should be co-facilitating the identification and articulation of the school mission while providing instructional leadership to staff in conjunction with the principal (Peterson and Kelley 2001). The administrative team, principal and assistant principal, should be working together to focus on common assessments, core standards, student work that should impact student growth, better teaching strategies, and student-data analysis (DuFour and Marzano 2009).

Principals need to facilitate the assistant principals' learning and mentor their skill-set development in the areas of budgeting, school-culture development, consistent evaluation strategies, curriculum development, and student learning (Peterson and Kelley 2001).

INTEGRATING THEORY INTO PRACTICE

The assistant-principal position is a dichotomy of roles and responsibilities. The assistant takes the position as a means to gain experience in leadership, and eventually glean his or her own building from this experience. The principal hires the assistant to take over a narrow description of duties, to take some responsibility off of the principal's shoulders so he or she can move forward on the district initiatives that have been established. With these assumptions in mind, both the principal and the assistant suffer from the challenge of moving the organization ahead and meeting individual, district, and student goals.

In reality, if you as the principal do not have the time to mentor the assistant, then setting the assistant up with an unofficial mentor in the form of a veteran staff member or contact from a local university may help in the skill development of the new administrator. The assistant should not feel isolated from his or her principal. The two should act in tandem, so a united message goes out to staff members, students, and parents.

When this does not occur, the assistant tends to seek out his or her own peers or companionship with staff members, which can create problems if one of these staff members is on the list to be evaluated by the assistant principal. The focus of the evaluation may not show any improvement because of the friendship or the awkward relationship when evaluating the friend as a teacher.

Discipline is usually a mainstay of the assistant principal's responsibilities. The assistant principal should request a copy of every teacher's classroom-behavior plan to ensure that the rules being followed are consistent with school and board policy. These plans are usually sent home with the students in the beginning weeks of school by the classroom teachers, to be signed by parents. If the plans do not meet school or board guidelines, then the assistant principal should share that information with his or her principal, and meet individually with that teacher in assisting with the necessary changes to ensure that the plan is consistent with current practice within the district and the building.

The plans of every teacher should be copied and filed with the assistant, so that if he or she is dealing with student-behavior issues it can be verified that the behavior is consistent with the rules that the teacher has established, in conjunction with board or school policy and/or guidelines.

Often teachers will only share the negative student and building issues with the assistant principal. That is why it is essential that an assistant have an open, constructive, healthy relationship with his or her principal and have an outside mentor to assist in problem-solving many of the issues that arise as the school year begins. The assistant role becomes very negative in regard to the student and parent community if he or she only deals with discipline. This will create rapid burnout for the assistant.

The assistant principal's perception of the principal's leadership style must be openly discussed within their initial partnership meeting so that the assistant can avoid unintentional conflict by marching off in a different direction. The perception of how the assistant principal visualizes himself or herself in the assistant role is also critical in their joint relationship and leadership style. The assistant needs to feel the support of the principal in working through problems and conflicts with staff members, students, and parents. Without the principal's support, the assistant's image could be damaged in the eyes of the stakeholders, and their perception becomes their reality.

Therefore, it is essential that the principal and the assistant principal work together and not in isolation. For the building administrators to work together in philosophy and be consistent in working through disciplinary issues assists in removing the personal prejudices that either administrator may feel toward a student or a parent because of repeat behaviors or offenses.

Administrator teamwork prevents and resolves potential conflicts and readies the assistant for his or her own principalship, and that is one of the reasons for the position. The assistant principal should be more than just a middle manager and be more of a cutting-edge leader, with the building principal's assistance.

CASE STUDIES

- You are a new principal with a veteran assistant who has been in the building and district for years. Your assistant has definite ideas of his or her job responsibilities, and has the support of many of the staff members who have been around a long time also. He or she has outlived the tenure of many building leaders at this high school. You want to change procedures and responsibilities, as discussed by your supervisor in your second interview with the superintendent. *How do you handle this situation?*
- You are a new assistant principal, and you feel very much alone and isolated. You were given your duties and responsibilities by the veteran principal, and were told by the principal how ineffective your predecessor was because of failing to follow the assigned-job-duty list. You now have your marching orders, and this is not what you were expecting to have signed up for in this new position. *What is your next move?*
- School has started and you, as a new assistant principal in a new building, are continuing to receive student office referrals for student behaviors that you feel should and could be handled in the classroom. There is a line at your door. The sending teacher is the president of the teaching association. *What do you do, and why are you doing it?*

CHAPTER REFLECTIONS

- Examining the assistant principalship from the perspective of a new principal inheriting a veteran assistant principal can reveal issues. One way to view this is as an opportunity to determine how to partner with this professional so that you can become a team. Keep in mind that it must be very threatening to have someone new come in and change what you have been doing as the assistant principal for years. You must take this into consideration when attempting to make changes. Sometimes you have to give to get, so you might ask the assistant what he or she has liked in the position and what he or she has not liked, and see if you can work through his or her dislikes by reorganizing some of the responsibilities. This will get you some initial buy-in from your new partner.

- Another way to view the assistant principalship is from the perspective of the new assistant. You will have taken all of the course work and learned different types of leadership theory, and now you have the opportunity to apply what you have learned. As a new assistant you are very excited and nervous and want to do a good job. Talking with your principal should give you some insight as to your responsibilities and obligations. If you are in charge of discipline, make sure you review all discipline procedures for each classroom. You can do this by collecting each teacher's opening information and syllabus; these are sent home for parents during the first few days of school. This may intimidate some of the veterans, as they may not have anything in writing, or perhaps they do not want some new administrator reviewing their information. If you let the teachers know you are doing this so you can support them, you may get better feedback. Working with your principal will help in this endeavor.

- Talk to your principal about what type of communication system you will have with him or her. Will you meet weekly as a team, or are you on your own? If you are on your own, make contact with other assistant principals within the district, and find someone you can talk to on a regular basis or someone who can mentor you through the difficult times ahead. Being proactive in this way will assist you in not making impulsive mistakes at the beginning. The assistant principalship is not an easy road to follow, but the experience will be very beneficial in the long run in your career. If you are just dealing with discipline issues in your role, try to find some other responsibility that will allow you access to students who do not regularly get into trouble. This avoids negativity and burnout.

REFERENCES

Bloom, G., and M. Krovetz. 2001. "A Step into the Principalship." *Leadership* 30, no. 3, 12–13.

DuFour, R., and R. Marzano. 2009. "High-Level Strategies for Principal Leadership." *ASCD Educational Leadership* 66, no. 5, 62–68.

Peterson, K., and C. Kelley. 2001. "Transforming School Leadership." *Leadership* 30, no. 3, 8–11.

Rooney, J. 2003. "Principals Who Care: A Personal Reflection." *Educational Leadership* 60, no. 6, 76–78.

West, C. 2011. "School Leadership Teaming." *NAESP Principal*, January–February, 10–13.

Chapter Four

The Elementary Principal

THEORY

Though the age level of a student varies from grade to grade and school to school, the competencies of a school leader remain constant. The refinement of these skill sets as they relate to the ages and grade levels of the school population determines the effectiveness of each leader at each level. The principal sets the tone and the atmosphere of a school for learning. The building leader is the connection between the school and the community of parents and stakeholders. The attitude, aptitude, and past experience of the principal impact the teaching and learning capacity of the teachers and students .

Statisticians and action researchers have indicated that there is a correlation between the success of students on high-stakes achievement tests and what a building leader does or does not do to impact the teaching and learning in his or her school prior to the assessment being given (Lomotey 1989). So a principal who is knowledgeable and proactive in early-childhood education can have a dramatic positive impact on achievement in later grades. The National Association for the Education of Young Children (1991) claims that building leaders must have a personal background in early-childhood development and education to make the appropriate decisions regarding the successful teaching of, and successful programming for, young children.

Prior to looking at programming, an elementary principal must consider the culture of his or her building. Many researchers have identified the following components of school culture as particularly important to student integration: student relationships with teachers, with peers, and the administration; safety; and warmth (Paredes 1993). The integration goes back to building relationships with other students, teachers, and administrators. The relationships create a culture or environment of belonging and a feeling of safety and human warmth. It is through this belonging that a person becomes resilient and academically successful.

Resilient children usually display characteristics of social competence, which is the ability to elicit positive responses from others (Christianson 1997). These students have a strong sense of identity and display a strong sense of purpose and have future goals (Krovetz 1999). Brooks (1998) completed a study describing the methodology in fostering a child's self-esteem and self-resilience, another form of resiliency. Resilient children need to have adults in their lives who focus on their islands of competencies rather than focusing on their weaknesses or utilizing pessimistic labels to describe children who are struggling.

Children who are resilient appear to have more advanced problem-solving and decision-making abilities than children who do not display these assets. Resilient children seem to make the connection between a positive self-image and positive school achievement. These children all appear to have the presence of a positive adult role model in their lives, whether it is a teacher, a counselor, or an administrator. It is the building leader's responsibility to create an atmosphere that welcomes new members to the learning community and creates a culture that is caring and connected (Sergiovanni 1992). It is obvious that the principal must take the lead in establishing this resiliency-encouraging climate and culture within his or her building if a student is truly going to be positively impacted and scholastically successful.

Once a positive culture of success has been established, the principal must determine what principles are necessary for instructional success. "Literacy coaching" is the new buzz phrase of the last decade. It is a means of imbedding continuous staff development within the daily routine of the classroom teaching within the building (L'Allier and Elish-Piper 2010). Research on coaches has determined that the success of a teacher coaching other instructors in his or her building depends upon the teacher's prior knowledge of content and prior successful implementation of that content in practice. Other research has focused on the roles and responsibilities of the teacher coach (Blachowicz, Obrochta, and Fogelberg 2005).

Most of the responsibility of the coach is focused on assisting teachers with classroom instruction. A coach must have the background knowledge and practice of assessment and prescriptive strategies to enhance instructional practice, as well as a strong understanding of literacy education (Frost and Bean 2006). The coach also has to be able to establish nonthreatening relationships with the teachers being coached. If an instructor feels threatened in any way by the teacher coach, the experience will not be effective (Flaherty 2005). L'Allier and Elish-Piper (2007) reported that the most effective teachers, associated with the highest averages in student literacy gains, were supported and coached by teacher coaches who held a reading teaching endorsement and an advanced degree. The opposite was also true, in that the lowest achievement results were associated with teachers coached by literacy coaches who did not have a reading endorsement or an advanced degree.

This is important research for the building leader to consider if he or she is going to institute literacy coaching in his or her building. Instead of selecting the contractual head teacher, or a supportive teacher within the building, as the coach, a building principal needs to look at the educational background, licensure, and success of the possible candidates and their individual teacher practice. A high skill level and strong personal interactions are two key components of selecting a prime candidate as a literacy coach.

Another aspect of positive student achievement that many elementary principals may be taking for granted or overlooking is class composition and the formation of annual classroom rosters at the start of every school year (Burns and Mason 2002). Burns and Mason (2002) claim to have found evidence that the methodology of building annual class rosters by grade level will directly impact student achievement outcomes. Sending and receiving teachers collect information on the students transitioning to the next grade level, taking into account learning modalities, future teacher instructional approaches and instructional strategies and techniques, and special needs of the students (whether learning needs or gifted/acceleration concerns), and construct class rosters without assigning a particular teacher or looking at student names.

The principal then takes those rosters and assigns them to specific instructors to accommodate better matches between learning needs and teacher instructional techniques and teacher practice (Monk 1987). When an imbalance occurs because of a transient student, the list may be altered over the summer by the building leader. As an elementary principal, you can take nothing for granted in determining the success of students in your building.

School climate, instructional management, curriculum design, and staff development must be priorities for the building leader in order to promote successful student achievement. Continual communication with parents is essential, and continually self-assessing the success of the building strategies you are implementing will make your elementary school one of the leading buildings within your district and/or state—and, more importantly, make student success the priority in all building decisions.

INTEGRATING THEORY INTO PRACTICE

Many times principals are hired for or transferred to elementary buildings when they have little to no experience with teaching that age level. Central-office administrators sometimes feel that young children are easy to manage and, apart from an occasional behavior to deal with in the office, the buildings for the most part seem to run themselves. This is a dangerous premise for any administrator looking forward to academic success within that elementary building.

Sensitivity to the needs of the students and building staff is essential in developing a strong class list and a strong academic schedule. Special-area teachers often develop their schedules first because the specialists travel between buildings and want to ensure that all classes are covered and taught in an efficient manner. This means that without considering the needs of the rest of the building, the times of the day that reading, language arts, and math can be taught are based upon the times that have been scheduled for art, music, and physical education. Though these classes are important, literacy must always come first.

Sometimes grade levels schedule reading and language arts first thing in the morning without consulting the special-education-intervention teachers, the speech-and-language pathologists, the occupational therapists, the adaptive-physical-education teachers, or the gifted-and-talented-intervention specialists, which means that the at-risk students are the last group scheduled by these instructors. This type of scheduling system does not take into consideration or allow time for co-teaching, double-dosing students in areas of need and remediation, or any type of positive intervention, and ultimately it will impact the literacy skill sets and scores of those at-risk students within your building.

Utilizing specialists with standardized assessment tools in the building the first week of school will greatly assist classroom teachers in benchmarking students in reading fluency, reading comprehension, and math computation. This allows the school to determine by grade level, based upon current baseline data, the most at-risk readers and math students within the building, and can assist in determining the content, types, and scheduling of interventions for the first quarter. From that point on, progress monitoring every six weeks must become a part of every classroom intervention. All students, based upon individual assessment and individual progress, should have the opportunity to move fluidly between tiers of intervention. Scheduling parents as extra eyes and ears can assist with simple scripted interventions, to help classroom teachers continue to monitor progress, and to help many of the students who are struggling but do not qualify for extra assistance.

Collaboration time is another scheduling priority for the building leader. In order to initiate or continue best practice in teaching, and allowing time for literacy coaching, coaches and teachers must be freed up for discussion, professional learning, and observation and staff development. All professional development needs to be connected to student achievement and student growth, based upon the literacy needs of your school and district initiatives.

Every elementary school needs a positive-behavior support program to assist students in feeling comfortable and safe in their learning environment. It should be an underlying positive current that is developed and taught intentionally by the building principal and the staff members. Every classroom and hallway, including the cafeteria, should incorporate that theme. A parent or stranger walking into the building should feel that sense of belonging and comfort from the program that is implemented. Students, as well as faculty and staff, should be able to speak about the program and how it impacts the culture of the building. All discipline should reflect the program, ensuring that every person is respected by all members of the school family.

All of the chapters in this book reflect the needs of building leaders kindergarten through twelfth grade. The implementation of these theories and themes needs to reflect the personality of the building leader and the culture of the school and district. The leader must always keep in mind that students and parents are the customers, and the reason that all principals, leaders, and teachers have their current positions. Using this philosophy helps keep everyone focused on the perspective that teaching and learning are the primary reasons for the existence of their employment.

CASE STUDIES

- After you have posted class lists but before the first day of school, a parent comes into your office and demands to have her child's teacher changed. The child's sibling had to endure this teacher—very unsuccessfully—and the parent will not tolerate another year of this type of misery for her family. She will go to the board of education and the superintendent if you do not grant her request. *As a new leader, how do you handle this type of concern, and what ramifications can your decision create for you in the future?*
- A parent has requested that her child be retested for the gifted-and-talented program. According to the parent, last year's principal had told her that her child would be assessed before school began, so that her child did not miss any instruction. There are no notes from the previous administrator, and last year's teacher was not privy to any conversation between the principal and the parent. The board guidelines suggest that all testing be completed in the spring, and in October. The parent request does not reflect this board philosophy, but the parent insists that you comply with the previous administrator's promise. *As a new principal, how do you stay consistent with board guidelines, but also meet the needs of the child and the parent demands?*

- The special-education-intervention teacher comes to you, explaining that the third-grade teacher insists that the entire special-needs population deficient in reading be removed from the reading class during reading instruction, and taken to a resource-room setting. The other teachers have allowed the children to stay in their classrooms, and the intervention teacher has been able to do some co-teaching and work in the back of the room with small groups. The third-grade teacher has tenure and is a very vocal union person in your building, and within the district. She continues to speak out about academic freedom of classroom teachers. *How do you, as a new principal, meet the needs of the children, and avoid a grievance in the process?*

CHAPTER REFLECTIONS

- Beginning as a new elementary principal can involve countless hours of preplanning, along with research as to what has occurred in the past. Reviewing student data, including past state scores, would be a good starting place for determining current student needs. Talking to veteran staff members who may have sat in on the interviews may give you quick insight into the needs of the building.
- Setting a realistic schedule that takes into account the needs of the students and current contractual language will assist you in developing a schedule that is workable and in the best interests of the students.
- Researching current assessments utilized in the district to benchmark and monitor progress will determine the amount of assistance necessary to benchmark and identify the lowest 25 percent reading, writing, and math students within your building. This data, compared to last year's state-test results, will be a good indicator of the needs of many of the children in your building, and will help the teachers intervene immediately to assist the struggling students.
- Most elementary schools have a positive-support program in place. Not changing everything at once may make your life easier as a new leader, and you may glean more staff support. However, if no one can define the program, ask some teacher leaders to come in before school starts to brainstorm and develop a positive program if one is lacking in the building.

REFERENCES

Blachowicz, C. L. Z., C. Obrochta, and E. Fogelberg. 2005. "Literacy Coaching for Change." *Educational Leadership* 62, no. 6, 55–58.

Brooks, R. 1998. "To Foster Children's Self-Esteem and Resilience, Search for Islands of Competence." *Brown University Child and Adolescent Behavior Letter* 14, no. 6.

Burns, R., and D. Mason. 2002. "Class Composition and Student Achievement in Elementary Schools." *American Education Research Journal* 39, no. 1, 207–33.

Flaherty, J. 2005. *Coaching: Evoking Excellence in Others*. 2nd ed. Burlington, MA: Elsevier Butterworth-Heinemann.

Frost, S., and R. Bean. 2006. *Qualifications for Literacy Coaches: Achieving the Gold Standard*. At www.literacycoachingonline.org/briefs/LiteracyCoaching.pdf (accessed September 7, 2011).

Krovetz, M. "Fostering Resiliency." 1999. *Sociological Collection* 28, no. 5, 1–5.

L'Allier, S. K., and L. Elish-Piper. 2009. Literacy Coaching in Three School Districts: Examining the Effects of Literacy Coaching on Student Reading Achievement." Paper presented at the annual conference of the International Reading Association, Minneapolis.

Lomotey, K. 1989. *African-American Principals: School Leadership and Success*. New York: Greenwood Press.

Monk, D. 1987. "Assigning Elementary Pupils to Their Teachers." *Elementary School Journal* 88, no. 2, 167–87.

Paredes, V. 1993. "School Correlates with Student Persistence to Stay in School." Paper presented at the annual meeting of the American Educational Research Association, Atlanta. ERIC Document Reproduction Service no. ED 359599.

Sergiovanni, T. 1992. *Moral Leadership: Getting to the Heart of School Improvement*. San Francisco: Jossey-Bass.

Chapter Five

Relationships

THEORY

Relationships are the most important aspect of the principal's role and success within a school. The connection the principal has with all stakeholders—administrators, athletic director, counselors, teaching staff, students, parents, support staff, and the local community—will eventually determine if the school is an effective learning environment. Principals cannot begin by giving directives if they want to establish relationships. Best practice is something that needs to be learned together as a staff (Donaldson et al. 2009). Best practice includes building a team culture of learners.

This team can only be established by creating a shared sense of being and purpose within the school program and culture. Creating this type of atmosphere and culture is based solely upon the individual relationship between the leader of the building and his or her constituents. Job satisfaction is created and principal effectiveness is generated when human emotions and relationships are the initial driving force of the new leader (Donaldson et al. 2009).

Once relationships are initiated and developed, the core focus of the school can be on increasing student achievement and student learning. This goal can be accomplished through shared decision making and shared ownership in the problems and the successes. Schools need to be perceived by all stakeholders as communities working together for a common cause. This negates the individual initiatives and creates a more group-focused agenda based upon a common bond (Ozgan 2011).

There is a strong correlation between an individual's perception and his or her individual behavior. The relationships between these individuals within an organization will have a direct impact on the behavior of the group. The building principal can exert control over those initial behaviors, and how they impact the school climate, by choosing how to frame his or her leadership style, and choosing how open, warm, and welcoming he or she will be from the beginning.

The principal who values, supports, and coaches stakeholders, initially and throughout his or her tenure, will instill hope, appreciation, and dedication in the culture (Yariv 2009). This dedication will produce positive student outcomes and positive support from staff members, students, and parents. As a novice administrator, it is imperative that you have a written plan of entry, and a strategy of how to effectively communicate initially to achieve buy-in and acceptance from staff members (Jentz 2009). First impressions go a long way in overall acceptance by staff members.

"Transparency" has become a colloquialism in politics and in schools. Community members want to be aware of and a part of what happens behind the school walls between eight and three every day, since their children are within those boundaries (Gordon and Louis 2009). A new principal needs to reach out to all families in both a face-to-face and technological manner, making those constituents feel welcome and a part of the school environment, and sharing new information.

Students want to feel safe and included as a part of the school culture. Students want the opportunity to participate in a large enough environment that they can each find their niche, yet they want the school to feel small enough that no one gets lost in the crowd. Again, the leadership within the building generates this feeling and culture. Principals must listen, recognize student concerns, and create action strategies to alleviate the problems (Donaldson et al. 2009). A building leader needs to participate in determining the needs and concerns of the building culture, and be an active part of resolving those problems, together with the learning community. This will create a team mentality.

Once relationships begin to develop and members of the learning community feel acknowledged and recognized in a positive light by the principal, then facilitation and consensus building can begin. Mediating problems can only occur after relationships have been established by the principal (Donaldson et al. 2009). The most successful building principal initially has his or her focus on people and attempting to establish honest and open relationships with all stakeholders.

INTEGRATING THEORY INTO PRACTICE

Relationship development is the most important aspect of the principalship position for a new administrator. This requires a great amount of time, commitment, and patience on the part of you, the new principal. New initiatives need to wait. E-mail and other managerial-type tasks also need to wait until after the school day, so that the proper concentration can be given to establishing relationships within the learning community. Individual and small-group or department conversations are essential to success.

The new administrator should begin, after initial conversations with the secretary and the custodian, with the assistant principal and the athletic director, both separately and together over the first few days. Sometimes sharing a meal is a great ice-breaker. It is very tempting, as the new person who is excited about starting a new position, to want to do all of the talking. After a brief introduction and a short review of your credentials, start asking questions and listen. You are going to be working with these people very closely; start to get to know them as people, not positions. By understanding their backgrounds you will understand how they can help your team be successful.

Listening is very difficult to do at initial meetings, as the new principal wants to share ideas and make changes. Do not make that mistake. Just listen. Notes should be written down after the meeting in private, summarizing what you've been told regarding past concerns, fears, or building or athletic issues and needs. Utilize that summary, and compare it to the concerns that were shared by the other stakeholders you have already met. This will give you a starting place to informally assess the past culture, and maybe generate some new ideas of where to begin with this staff. Remember, these administrators are checking you out as you are doing the same to them. The only issue is, they have established relationships within the building and will share their fears and hopes about you with other staff members. Think about what you are willing to share before you meet with these key players.

The guidance counselors touch every aspect of the learning community. Students feel comfortable with them. Parents have developed a trusting relationship with them, knowing that they will advocate for their children. Teachers and custodians feel comfortable unloading their concerns with these professionals. The counselor is another key player within the culture to befriend. He or she has an established track record for being compassionate, organized, and a trusted listener.

It is essential that you meet this professional and develop a comfortable rapport. He or she could be your best ally and biggest cheerleader when talking with other stakeholders. Counselors are often viewed as quasi-administrators. Take time to determine how the counseling department works, and how you want it to work. This can often be a place to make small changes, if handled correctly, and these changes can affect the entire building. Asking the counselors to generate a list of every student in the building, and having teachers highlight the names of students with whom they've established relationships, will give you and the staff the needed information as to who has no relationship with an adult in the building, and then you can consider who will begin to reach out to these children.

Orchestrating a meeting with senior or upper-class student leaders to seek out their concerns and allow them to get to know you will assist in establishing order on that first day of school. Seeking out what they like and don't like about the school will be good information to compare to your notes from other constituents. Explain that as the principal, you want to organize a student forum and meet with this forum on a regular basis to hear concerns and problem-solve. This is how respect is initially established with the student body. Students will share the outcome of the meeting with other classmates. Word of mouth can be the new administrator's best friend, if the meetings go well.

Gather the names and numbers of the booster presidents and leaders and establish a meeting with them as soon as possible. Introduce yourself, but again just listen. This will provide community information and input regarding the problems that have occurred, and the hopes of the parental community for the future with this new administration. Again, write down the positives and the negatives after the meeting, and begin to look for common themes, or common perceptions about the school and the school community.

Usually at this point the new principal is overwhelmed and begins to question the sanity of taking the new position. This is typical, and it will pass once the list of concerns can be prioritized with the assistance of the stakeholders. Remember, establishing relationships while gleaning information is the purpose of the meetings. The problems did not occur overnight and will not be remedied for quite some time. There is no pressure, other than what a person puts on himself or herself initially.

The custodians and cafeteria workers and monitors feel very much neglected in the school community. Many feel they are perceived as second-class citizens because they do not have degrees or the skill sets of the other professionals within the building. However, this group of employees will make the building and the cafeteria and the classrooms run smoothly, or they can create a chaotic problem for the new principal. Give these employees the same time and respect that have been given to the other stakeholder groups. Listening to this group will give the new principal great insight into what's working and what is not working in the classrooms and lounges throughout the facility. Again, summarize that information.

Finally, meet with the superintendent to get an idea of his or her expectations for you and the administrative role, the goals for the school and faculty, and any problems or concerns that are his or her priority. That would be a great time to share some of the summary informational themes that you have gathered throughout the multiple meetings that have occurred throughout the past two weeks, and notice his or her agreement or disagreement regarding what has been discovered. This adds direction and tentative timelines to the goals for the beginning of the year. It is difficult to believe that school has not even started yet.

These meetings have inaugurated an acquaintance type of relationship with many of the key players within the community. What these community members like and dislike will be shared throughout the rest of the community by word of mouth. Maintain an open-door policy so that constituents can come and visit throughout the final weeks of summer. Ensure that the regular correspondence, e-mails, phone calls, and meetings are dealt with in a timely manner. This may mean some late nights at the start of the new position.

These first couple of weeks will be exhausting, and the start of the school year will look better and better because all of these people will then have classes to teach, classes to attend, phones to answer, and buildings to clean. This, however, is the most essential time for the new administrator to set the tone for how he or she wants the climate of the building to begin to develop. Small conversations and quick smiles go a long way in establishing rapport with the leadership style the new administrator wants to establish within the building and the community. Once the school year begins, the focus can begin to shift to teaching and learning.

CASE STUDIES

- A parent calls and leaves you a phone message on your second day in the job, and before you can return the call she shows up first thing in the morning. She is very angry. This is your first meeting with this parent, who you find out is very active in numerous booster groups for the school. Her adolescent has been cut from the varsity soccer squad because he is academically ineligible because of grades. Last June he had incompletes, and the previous principal and classroom teacher said she would take the late work and give him credit. The parent tells you he has been ill. The incompletes have now turned into failing grades, making him ineligible. Your athletic director, according to the parent, was very rude to her at the first scrimmage, in front of many parents and students, and would not allow her son to play. She continues on by saying the athletic director has always had it in for her son. The first game is in two days. You have already heard from a board member about the issue with the athletic director. *What are you going to do to rectify this situation?*

- You have left your door open to encourage and model an open-door poli-cy. Teachers and staff members have been streaming in and out, making requests to the point where you feel like the Godfather. One teacher told you he would miss opening day to visit a parent. The previous principal said it would be OK. Another teacher demands to have her room moved, as promised last year by the previous administration. Another teacher is concerned because her software and books were not ordered in time as promised, and now will not arrive until three weeks after school starts. These are her lesson plans. *How do you handle these requests individual-ly?*
- A parent comes in angry and unannounced before school begins, because her counselor will not change her daughter's schedule. The parent's other child had the same teacher and, according to the parent, he does not like her family. The teacher bullied her other daughter, and nothing was done about it. The parent tells you that the teacher does not like adolescents. The counselors, according to the parent, charge for any schedule change. The parent offered to write a check, but the counselor claimed she would not change schedules for a convenience move, but only for class conflicts. *How do you resolve the issue, and how can you account for or justify the charging of money for a student schedule change in a public school? Where does that money go?*

CHAPTER REFLECTIONS

- As a new principal or assistant principal, the best and most important step you can take is building relationships with the people you will be working with on a daily basis. Change cannot occur if you do not have the trust of your stakeholders. Building trust is not an overnight accomplishment. Your employees, your students, and your parents are going to initially take a "wait and see" attitude toward your leadership style. They want to see who you are and what you expect, and if you walk the talk of your philosophy of leadership.
- Building trust with staff members happens in mostly informal settings. The survey you disseminated gives the staff an idea that you value their input, but only if you show you are using the information that they shared with you. There may be an outlier in the staff with one pet concern who, if this concern is not addressed—regardless of its practicality—can cause major damage with the rest of the staff. It is important to address all of the issues, even if it means explaining why something cannot be done. Letting staff know that you will support them in conferences or in public when they are under attack, but will deal with the issues of concern privately,

will also bolster your reputation. Though this sounds calculating, attempt to build relationships with the leaders in your building, starting with your assistant principal and other administrators and guidance counselors, to ensure you have a team of support. Your best and worst friend will be word of mouth, so building relationships is essential to making any dramatic changes within your building.

- Follow-through is also essential in building relationships. Staff and students are going to watch to see if you follow through with what you initially said you were going to do, whether it is giving feedback from the survey you distributed, being in the hallways during class changes, keeping meetings on time, or getting the items that you promised to teachers. Everyone will have a "wait and see" attitude with you, so you are in the driver's seat as far as ensuring that you are consistent and outgoing with your staff.

REFERENCES

Donaldson, G., G. Marnik, S. Mackenzie, and R. Ackerman. 2009. "What Makes or Breaks a Principal." *Educational Leadership* 67, no. 2, 8–14.

Gordon, M., and K. Louis. 2009. "Linking Parent and Community Involvement with Student Achievement: Comparing Principal and Teacher Perceptions of Stakeholder Influence." *American Journal of Education* 116, 1–31.

Jentz, B. 2009. "First Time in a Position of Authority." *Kappan* 91, no. 1, 56–60.

Ozgan, H. 2001. "The Relationships between Organizational Justice, Confidence, Commitment, and Evaluating the Manager and the Perceptions of Conflict Management at the Context of Organizational Behavior." *Educational Sciences: Theory and Practice* 11, no. 1, 241–47.

Yariv, E. 2009. "The Appraisal of Teachers' Performance and Its Impact on the Mutuality of Principal-Teacher Emotions." *School Leadership and Management* 29, no. 5, 445–61.

Chapter Six

Communication

THEORY

Communication is the "mainframe" of the school. The more a principal listens, the better he or she will communicate with teachers, students, parents, and staff members. Listening requires paying close attention to the words that teachers, parents, students, and staff members and others use, as well as their body language while sharing, and the tone with which they communicate their wants, needs, and complaints on a daily basis (Rooney 2008). It is very easy when listening to jump to an impulsive problem-solving mode, when sometimes people just need to vent, and are not looking for specific solutions. Administrators need to study informal and formal data and past practice before rendering any decisions.

Communication does not have to be and should not be just a one-to-one conversation. Technology has both assisted and hindered the flow of information within a building and school community. Principals have a wealth of digital tools at their fingertips with which to engage the school community. These tools, and they are just tools, can create a major problem or avert a major crisis. Too many scattered e-mails can appear fragmented over a week, and the messages may become lost in the sheer number of word bites (Buck 2010). The tone of e-mails may also cause concern or send the wrong message.

Some principals are composing weekly blogs, sharing information from the previous week as well as information about the upcoming week, with links to research articles on best practices as they tie in to a particular blog topic. Blogs are becoming more and more popular because they are free, quick and easy, and "twenty-first century," and they can reach the constituents anytime and anywhere and can be saved forever.

Blogs also work in the other direction. Principals need to be aware that parents also are having conversations on blogs, message boards, or Listservs in the community away from the school (Porterfield and Carnes 2010). A principal needs to be able to tap into this information to know what the perceptions are outside of the four walls of the building. Search engines can assist in locating this information.

Many administrators are using social media such as Facebook and Twitter to communicate to constituents. Technology is a wonderful tool to reach the community, but it cannot be the only means of communication. A strong principal shoots many arrows at one target to get his or her message across. Face-to-face meetings still need to be a priority in meeting the needs of stakeholders. Teachers, parents, and especially students want to be recognized by name so that they feel important to the school administrator and the school. Sometimes taking a yearbook from the previous year home and studying names will assist in this endeavor.

Business is not the same as it was in education in the past. Schools are competing for a customer base, and parents have many options besides the neighborhood school. Principals must communicate to teachers that the students are the customers, and the teachers' positions cannot be guaranteed anymore without the appropriate number of students and the appropriate funding available annually. Communication is the key to staying in business.

Principals must leave their offices and be in the halls, the lunchroom, and the classrooms. Many parents have started subgroups based on shared interests, such as a group for parents of children who are on individualized education programs, which may be an offshoot of a problem that had risen after an administrative decision had been rendered. These groups may be meeting over breakfast at a local restaurant or coffee bar, and not even using technology to communicate their needs, and thus they may be inaccessible unless a connection can be made by the leader of the building.

Administrators must be aware of their audiences. Each parent, student, or teacher department may have different needs. One message stated in the same manner may not be appropriate for all stakeholders, whatever the medium. Principals need to ask the community members what type of tool they want utilized to share information. There will always need to be more than one tool or form of communication on the same topic.

Many times staff members will catch a principal in the hallway on the run and ask for clarification of, or a ruling on, a certain topic (Gronn 1983). These can be dangerous waters for an administrator as a flip, off-the-cuff response can send the wrong message and create future issues within the building through word of mouth. Coming from the principal, words "mean more" and will be interpreted as gospel by all constituents.

A building principal must be strategic and direct in his or her responses when caught off guard. Taking the information down and getting back to the staff member after reviewing past practice may avert difficult consequences. There is a major difference between listening and hearing information. How the information is presented, including the tone and body language, should give the new administrator guidance on the nature of the request, complaint, or comment. Too often a principal wants to give a flippant or cursory response so as to move on to the next problem and get this one off his or her desk, without realizing that this same issue will arise again later on because the principal never fully listened in the first place.

Most administrators are former teachers who controlled their environment through the structure of lesson plans. There was teacher talk and solicited student talk. New principals must step out of this familiar role to be successful. Administrators are now facilitators of change, and not the "sage on the stage." They must partner with their stakeholders to make an impact, and to ensure that everyone is on the same page at the same time (Gronn 1983).

Timeliness is the last issue that can make or break a principal. Returning phone calls and e-mails and setting up timely appointments is essential to success. Callers want a personal phone call from the building leader, not a quick response from a secretary. Many conflicts can be avoided by the principal's listening to a concern on the other end of the phone. E-mail replies that follow some form of proper etiquette, with a greeting and a closing, will assist in public relations and demonstrate that this response is not just another thing crossed off the administrator's to-do list.

If a principal waits too long to communicate or act on a question or concern he or she has indirectly made a decision by not commenting, thus showing support for the status quo whatever that may be in a given situation (Young et al. 2008). If a principal fails to communicate to all of his or her constituents in a timely, accessible manner, he or she will short out the "mainframe" in the building and community and create a crisis out of a minor problem, which could have been avoided by listening and responding appropriately.

INTEGRATING THEORY INTO PRACTICE

All the information gleaned from the new administrator's first encounters with secretaries, custodians, assistant principals, the athletic director, teacher leaders, booster parent leaders, and student leaders should be compiled into a hierarchy of strengths, weaknesses, and concerns. This should be put into a document that can be circulated in a survey format to all stakeholders, so that they can rank their individual priorities. This survey can be a catalyst for beginning to gather informational needs as dictated by the constituents, for studying specific topics for the school year. The strategic plan of the central office or the district should also take priority in this endeavor.

Focus groups are a great venue for studying information. Many districts have late starts or early dismissals monthly or quarterly, to study specific issues within the district or the specific buildings. As a new administrator, you can orchestrate the topics by priority, as determined by the stakeholder survey. Teachers should sign up for the topics that they are passionate about, or the problems that they are very interested in finding a solution to in a group situation. Included in all of this data should be the disciplinary report from the year or from previous years, so that major disciplinary issues can also be addressed in a group by staff. Topics should be numbered by preference, so that every group has about seven to nine people participating in the study.

Focus groups should base their decision-making ability on research. Provide, if at all possible, one current peer-reviewed journal article on the topic that is being studied to begin the process in each focus group. This will give at least a couple of possible solutions that will be outside of the typical school culture. Often staff members begin and end a career in the same room and building. This lack of outside information and exposure stifles the creative problem-solving process, and limits the number of outside-the-box solutions to everyday problems. That is why it is imperative to get these teachers involved in the process.

These focus groups are more defined groups than the beginning groups at the start of the year. After reading research to narrow the topic, each group should write up a blog or notes to be shared with other staff members and stakeholders after meetings. This will allow for group input and prevent groups from working in isolation and going off on tangents that do not interest the rest of the faculty. Try also to include key classified-staff members, such as a secretary and/or a custodian, in these focus groups. After the principal has developed trust with the group, which could take years in some cases, it is a great idea to include a parent and a student in each group to ensure that all constituents are represented and have input.

Staff meetings are another source of strong or weak communication. Many meetings consist of sharing information that could have been sent out on the weekly blog post or memo. Staff meetings should follow a timed problem-solving format. Too much time should not be spent on discussing the problem; time should instead be devoted to developing solutions to that problem. Too often schools get lost in the complaints and negativity, and never resolve the issues. It just snowballs, and meetings become an ineffective way to communicate; and the negative comments and conversations find their way to the parking lot, away from the administrator's ears.

Developing the agenda should be a group process. There may be items percolating in the lounge that could be discussed at a staff meeting, items that the leader may not even be aware exist as issues in the building if he or she doesn't share the agenda items in advance and ask for input from staff members. Many buildings have building-committee meetings to discuss concerns, which usually are contract or union based. This may not be a constructive means of solving problems that everyone is concerned about; rather, the focus may be the concerns of one noisy rank-and-file member who continues to bring about the same concerns regularly to building representatives, who must share with administration.

Seating at staff meetings is an essential part of resolving issues. In large secondary buildings, there could be 100 teachers and staff members sitting in the cafeteria or auditorium—whichever room within the building will hold such a large population. Teachers tend to group by department or sit in groups of friends, and sit in the back of the room so that they can grade papers, make quiet comments, or read the sports page during the discussion. Arranging the room in a circle or square so that everyone can see everyone and no one is isolated in the back of the room helps facilitate constructive discussions.

Notes from all meetings, including parent meetings, should be shared with staff members so that there are no surprises. It is very awkward and difficult if a parent knows something that a staff member was not privy to in advance. Having instructors and students present different activities or projects that they are working on in class is a great way of sharing some of the best practices that are occurring in the building, and the parents will be thrilled to have that information.

Developing a strong parent group should lead to developing a strong volunteer network for school projects. In U.S. schools, parents are very involved with volunteering through sixth grade. Once a child becomes an adolescent, the teen tells the parent to stay away from school so that he or she (the student) is not embarrassed. This is the worst thing a parent can do for the child. Junior high through high school is the most vulnerable time for teens. Peer pressure and hormones run wild, and if a parent does not have a strong relationship and good communication with the secondary-school principal or teacher, the parent may be unaware what current popular trends or fads are running rampant through the hallway or the culture of the building that may cause the student to make poor decisions.

Attending events is one of the easiest but most time-consuming ventures of the principal. Parents and students want to see their building leader participating or watching during athletic events, competitions, club activities, and dances. This is a very time-consuming undertaking for the principal, and he or she should weekly if not monthly divide the activities among the administrators so that every event is covered. Events should be varied so that the principal can be seen in every venue, whether athletic or co-curricular in nature. The high-school principal often is the most visible person in the district. This voluntary participation is an excellent way for the principal to communicate informally with parents and students by showing his or her undivided attention to the attended activity.

Open houses, conferences, and award banquets show support but also provide opportunities for strong communication. A principal does not have to stay for the entirety of every event, but as long as he or she is recognized and communicates and can stay for part of the event, he or she can then leave and go on to another event (as there are usually multiple events in a given evening).

Conferences with parents who may be upset or angry regarding special-education needs or discipline actions are an occasion on which the principal needs to be playing his or her best game. The administrator must sift through any anger or grieving that the parent may be struggling with over the disability or issue, and listen for a potentially hidden concern that might be the true catalyst for the anger. The principal should watch body language, facial expressions, and "table behavior"—such as pushing back from the table, keeping the arms crossed, or making little to no eye contact—to get a feel for the concerns.

Often if the anger is directed at a staff member, that person gets defensive. Getting defensive is the worst thing that can happen in a meeting because the focus leaves the real issue and is transferred to another staff member, and the issue will get lost in that transfer. It is essential that the principal follow the mechanics of the discussion closely and lead that anger and transference back to the real issue, to develop problem-solving strategies that all can agree upon for trying to help the student be more successful. The anger at the teacher that has triggered the meeting might really have derived from the parent's desire to unload on the teacher for something that happened some time ago or in a different venue, like coaching. Remember, these adolescents are the parents' babies, no matter how physically large they appear to be.

Finally, if you, as the new school principal, utilize every digital, voice, and face-to-face communication tool available, and do so appropriately, there is a greater chance for success, and for creating a high-powered, user-friendly, positive, safe environment. This user-friendly environment will lead to a caring and trusting school culture for all stakeholders. Remember, relationships begin with communication and trust. The top schools in the country are schools that are built on strong relationships and trust. This trust will lead to change and impact teaching and learning positively and dynamically within the school environment.

CASE STUDIES

- A parent conference is scheduled because a parent is upset over her son's grades, and feels the teacher has been picking on her son all year. The teacher is very apprehensive and asks a union representative to sit in on the meeting with the parent, which dramatically changes the dynamics of the meeting. The parent asks a question, and the union representative answers instead of the teacher. Tempers are beginning to flare, and the conference is going downhill quickly. *What do you, as the principal, do to rescue the conference?*
- You, the principal, have held a departmental meeting regarding possible changes in the number of classroom sections offered next year, and you've requested that the department chairs keep the information confidential until it is determined by central office to be definite that some teachers may be part of a reduction in force, and that "bumping" could occur over the summer for the following school year. You return to your office an hour after the meeting, and there are teachers from different departments in your office and various e-mails on your e-mail page expressing concern about rumors of possible teacher layoffs next year. There are trust issues and confidentiality-violation issues within your building. *What can you do to resolve these issues?*
- According to the teacher contract, teachers may bid for positions from one building to another when a vacancy occurs. The principal has the right to not hire that person from the other building, but must justify his or her response in writing. A person has applied for a guidance-counselor position. The other counselors in your building have made it very clear to you how unhappy they would be working with this person. *What could you say or do to discourage this applicant from taking the position, or what could you do to encourage your staff members to accept this person as the new counselor?*

CHAPTER REFLECTIONS

- Communication is the key to your success as a principal. Even with all of the technology available, people want to see you and meet you. They want to feel that you are approachable, and that you lead by building relationships, and not by creating a fear factor around your presence. This can only be accomplished through visibility. Staying in your office, even with the door open, is not the same as being in the hallways, the cafeteria, the lounge, and the classrooms.

- Creating a communication system with your assistants and with your supervisor is a way to ensure that no one is ever surprised by information. Meeting with your assistant on a regular, predetermined basis is the only way to ensure you are giving out the same message about your leadership style. Have an informal agenda together so you stay on task, and do not turn the meeting into a gripe session. Communicating with your supervisor is another important factor. Principals need to ask supervisors what they would like to be informed about. Just like you don't want to be caught off guard, neither does your supervisor. Utilizing e-mail, or sending the supervisor a weekly update, will keep everyone informed and on the same page. Your weekly update may not get any feedback from your supervisor, but at least you know there will not be any surprises. If you think the supervisor will be getting a complaint or phone call about you, let the supervisor know in advance so that he or she will have the whole story before the call arrives. Communication will either make or break you as a leader.

REFERENCES

Buck, F. 2010. "Improve Communication One Blog at a Time." *NAESP Principal*, March–April, 54–55.

Gronn, P. 1983. "Talk as the Work: The Accomplishment of School Administration." *Administrative Science Quarterly* 28, 1–21.

Porterfield, K., and M. Carnes. 2010. "Tools of the Trade." *NAESP Principal*, March–April, 28–35.

Rooney, J. 2008. "What New (Young) Principals Need to Know." *Educational Leadership*, 84–85.

Young, S., W. Berube, and S. Perry. 2008. "The Influence of Technology on Communication for School Leaders: Preferences, Beliefs, and Use." *Planning and Changing* 39, nos. 1–2, 81–97.

Chapter Seven

Teaching and Learning

THEORY

Education in the United States is being overhauled to include a core curriculum of rigor. The accountability of districts, school administrators, and teachers goes hand in hand with this new curriculum. No longer can departments or instructors teach subject matter that they feel is important based upon generic state standards. With this new, rigorous core-curriculum accountability, critical thinking, collaboration, oral and written communication, and ability to analyze information and solve problems are being measured directly and indirectly through the common assessments (Wagner 2008).

In the past, teachers went into their subject matter because it was something they enjoyed while they were in school. The subject matter was presented in a verbal-learning format with a lecture, a discussion, and a weekly quiz or a summative assessment after a chapter. Homework figured into the grade, depending on the subject and the teacher's discretion. Instructors developed their own assessments or utilized assessments provided by the textbooks. Students received grades quarterly, and a summative exam for the course was given at the end of the semester, carrying a hefty grade-point weight. This was secondary education.

In public schools, principals would do a formal observation that was prearranged with the teacher, and from this information the principal would complete an evaluation. Departments would meet monthly, usually informally, and discuss issues within the department. The text was not usually used as a tool but rather as the scope and sequence for the course. Subject matter and content were more important than the presentation format and student learning.

With the new set of rules requiring them to utilize the core curriculum and making them accountable, teachers are now more interested in creating opportunities for their students to learn (Brookhart, Moss, and Long 2008). Teachers are taking a look at formative assessments. Formative assessments are a process, not a summative exam. It is a vehicle to give feedback on the teaching and the learning as students progress through instruction (Popham 2008). From the feedback that the instructor receives, he or she can adjust the lessons to meet the student's needs and to achieve the ultimate curricular standard.

Teachers are now talking about UDL, *universal design for learning*. This takes into account all learners' needs and examines the presentation of material, rather than just looking at subject content material. It provides a blueprint for designing lessons that meet the needs of all learners (Meo 2008). This lesson and presentation take into account all learning modalities and products and evidence of learning. Students are being asked to assist in formulating the problems, doing research, thinking critically, and communicating solutions utilizing various strategies and evidence, and they are also asked to be precise in their responses, through the strategies that best meet their learning needs (Conley 2011).

This is a major paradigm shift in secondary education. Students are now partnering with the teacher in learning. No longer is the teacher the only one who knows where the lesson is going. Together, teachers and students are sharing learning targets (Moss, Brookhart, and Long 2011). This translates into students who are empowered, motivated, and self-driven in meeting the goal. It promotes self-determination, authentic assessment, and collaboration (Villa et al. 2005).

Many principals now utilize a weekly walk-through system of observation, asking students during a lesson to state what the goal of the day's lesson is. This information is partnered with the formal observation to give feedback to the instructor. Education is now in a radical reform effort nationally. Principals are now looking at student data, professional development, common assessments, interventions, and administrative support to impact the best practice of teaching and learning (Bain 2010).

INTEGRATING THEORY INTO PRACTICE

These are exciting and frightening times for a building leader. Years ago, principals were told to just keep an eye on the "three *B*s": *buses* (transportation), *balls* (athletics), and *beans* (cafeteria). Now a principal is expected to be the instructional leader within the building, on top of the daily managerial needs of running a secondary facility. New principals may find their buildings in different stages of development in the reform initiative. Some may just be at the beginning, while others may be on their way to best practice. Still others may be trying to fight the change process altogether.

As the new person on the block, you may find that attending departmental meetings can give you insight into where everyone is in the process. In all probability, each department will be in a separate phase of reform. It is your job to facilitate the transition for those teachers and departments who do not want to change, and to not stand in the way of or stifle those teachers or departments who are on their way to best practice. It is almost as if you need to differentiate your expectations in this process for each teacher or department, depending on where they are in the process, expecting all to eventually reach the same best-practice teaching and learning goal.

As a starting point, classroom visits, not formal observations, will give you great insight as to how lessons are presented, whether teaching practice is current and innovative, and whether the teacher is partnering with the students in the learning process. You can do this in short five- to ten-minute visits and communicate with the students as to the goal or intent of the lesson, in the students' own words. By blocking out one period per day, you can get through twenty-five to fifty walk-throughs in a week. From this information, make informal notes about current practice in each classroom and department, and what sort of professional development is needed to take these instructors to the next level.

Meetings with department chairs and counselors offer another venue to discuss best practice and what is happening in the classroom. This is also a great forum in which to begin discussing common assessments between content classes. Teachers teaching AP courses already have a common assessment and curriculum. This is a great springboard to initiate that conversation about other classes and standardizing the assessment format. It also is a good opportunity to discuss presentation strategies within the departments.

If, based on your instructor observations, you have someone who has stood out in best practice or who is illustrating what you want to see in the classroom buildingwide, then offer a substitute—even if you have to sub it yourself—to allow other teachers the opportunity to observe such peers within the building. This is tender ground, and must be approached tactfully, as some teachers will feel threatened or ineffective as teachers if you ask them to go observe a peer. This is where building trust with the department chairs is essential, so you can have them approach other teachers within their departments to take a look at another approach or presentation style within the building.

With the current annual yearly progress regulations, it is imperative that you begin to think of interventions for those students who are unsuccessful. *Unsuccessful* does not just mean that they are failing classes; it also relates to their performance on standardized tests. Too often in secondary education, teachers and counselors do not review student files to determine what previous interventions were attempted in earlier grades to help the students be successful. When you check the signatures on the sign-in page of a secondary student's cumulative file, it is very common to see a fifth-grade teacher as the last person who went through the file. Reviewing a file provides great information to assist in intervening with learning difficulties or to get ideas on how previous teachers assisted the student. This should be the first step in intervening with any student.

It is also imperative that you look at student failures, at both the midquarter and the end of the quarter. Your guidance counselors should be able to provide that information for you by their individual caseloads. Calculate the number of failures for each teacher. Knowledge of what teacher appears to have the most failures is great information. Meeting and talking with each teacher about the number of failures and why each student was unsuccessful will also give you more information regarding that teacher's expectations and possible teaching practices. It will also provide you individual information on how a teacher grades and what the reason is for the failure(s). It could be lack of homework, poor test grades, absenteeism, or some other cause. Again, teaching should be a four-way partnership between the teachers, the students, the parents, and the building administrator.

Meeting with teachers provides another opportunity for you to get to know them on a personal level. This should not be a confrontational meeting, but rather a brainstorming session to look at grading and the importance of homework and how that is evaluated. Providing a research-based article on grading or on giving zeros for noncompletion of student work instead of giving the highest F possible is a great way to start a conversation. You will get opposition toward this point of view, but any discussion opens the door for change down the road and future reform initiatives.

Prior to beginning any observations, walk-throughs, or discussions about grades, make sure you have familiarized yourself with the teacher contract as it pertains to these points. Your good intentions could backfire if you are not familiar with what is acceptable and not acceptable within the contract. Contact another principal within the district for guidance in these areas. Remember that you cannot do everything at once, or you will get overwhelmed and accomplish nothing. Set some short-term and some long-term goals for yourself as to where you want to be by the end of the semester, and where you want to be at the same time next year. Stay focused on best practice and teaching and learning.

CASE STUDIES

- The assistant principal has completed an observation of a veteran social-studies teacher. The lesson appeared very dynamic, utilizing a springboard film clip, a cooperative learning exercise, and group discussion, and every student appeared to be engaged and to know the goal of the lesson. Nevertheless, the assistant principal was concerned: As the administrator was walking back to the office, several students stopped her and shared that they loved having the assistant in the classroom. They shared that this was the first time they had ever known what the goal of the lesson was for the day; also, they'd rarely had group work or discussions. It was an exciting lesson for them, because usually the teacher lectured and they took notes. *How do you handle this, or what do you recommend that the assistant share with the teacher?*
- The English-department chair comes to you with a concern: one of the new English teachers is giving very little or no feedback on student essays. She looked at some of the essays when she was supervising a study hall and could not believe that this teacher had given so many high grades for work that was unacceptable in her eyes. *What is a long-term solution for the inconsistencies in the department?*
- The guidance counselor shares that one science teacher in the building has given the most failing grades in the department for the quarter. The concern is that these students will fall behind on credits and will have a long-term risk of not graduating with their class. The counselor also shares that this has been going on for years, and it has never been addressed with the teacher. You meet with the teacher, and he claims the students cannot complete the math necessary for the class, and they score poorly on the assessments he creates for them. *What is the solution for the failing students?*

CHAPTER REFLECTIONS

- Teaching and learning are the most important aspects of your position. They are why you were hired as a building leader. Developing relationships with staff and communicating with staff are tools in the overall endeavor of impacting the teaching and learning that take place in your building. You have been trained in what good teaching looks like in the classroom. By participating in a walk-through of classrooms weekly, you will soon realize where your weak links are in the building. The leadership comes into play when you want to assist those teachers in becoming stronger educators.

- As a building principal working through the evaluation process, you cannot be "friends" with staff. You can build relationships and trust, but not in such a way that a friendship might compromise your ability to lead. You will lose friends over the evaluation process, and that is OK.
- Common assessments for all classes will ensure that every student is getting the same education. If you can eventually use some standardized, nationally normed assessment, you can get a good idea of how competitive and on-target your school is compared to others nationally. Developing a common building rubric for written composition and a common note-taking strategy buildingwide will assist in providing structure for every student. Remember, these strategies must be taught, and they should be posted in every room annually. Encouraging students to take AP classes and take the AP tests will also give you good feedback.
- Grading, formative assessments, and homework are very good focus-group topics. Make sure the research is available to the staff. As the leader you will want to provide that information. Include topical discussions on the common core, rigor, and good teaching practices. These are topics that should not be treated in isolation but instead connected to the building goals you have established as a school team. Remember, staff development must tie in to your goals, and at each training you should provide the connection for the staff as to how this all fits together to meet the building needs and goals. You may hear from some veteran teachers that they don't want to do this extra stuff. They just want to teach their subject content areas. In this case, remind the staff that you as a building leader will always be moving forward, and these are not educational fads that will go away. To be effective, teachers must stay current with the changes in the field—otherwise the teaching practice within the building will begin to stagnate. It is up to you, as the instructional leader of the building, to ensure that the current literature and trends in education are available to your staff members, and that they are educated in best practice.

REFERENCES

Bain, A. 2010. "A Longitudinal Study of the Practice Fidelity of a Site-Based School Reform." *Australian Educational Researcher* 37, no. 1.

Brookhart, S., C. Moss, and B. Long. 2008. "Formative Assessment That Empowers." *Educational Leadership* 66, no. 3.

Conley, D. "Building on the Common Core." 2011. *Educational Leadership* 68, no. 6.

Meo, G. 2008. "Curriculum Planning for All Learners: Applying Universal Design for Learning (UDL) to a High School Reading Comprehension Program." *Preventing School Failure* 52, no. 2.

Moss, C., S. Brookhart, and B. Long. "Knowing Your Learning Target." 2011. *Educational Leadership* 68, no. 6.

Popham, W. J. 2008. *Transformative Assessment*. Alexandria, VA: ASCD.

Villa, R., J. Thousand, A. Nevin, and A. Liston. 2005. "Successful Inclusive Practices in Middle and Secondary Schools." *American Secondary Education* 33, no. 3 (Summer).

Wagner, T. 2008. "Rigor Redefined." *Educational Leadership* 66, no. 2.

Chapter Eight

Response to Intervention

THEORY

Response to intervention (RTI) is a tiered approach to intervening with students who are struggling within the classroom. RTI uses this tiered approach to provide evidence-based strategies to assist these struggling students throughout their instruction. Students may go in and out of intervention, depending upon the concept that they may be struggling with during instruction. Instructors need to use benchmarking or some form of formative assessment to measure the learning success of the students (Canter, Klotz, and Cowan 2008).

There are three tiers in RTI. Tier 1 consists of using universal best practice and evidence-based strategies with all students within the classroom. The instructor designs research-based strategies that will help struggling students learn a concept that may be more difficult for them to master.

Tier 2 involves modifications and accommodations to assist those students who are still struggling in understanding the concept or skill set. These students are usually worked with in small groups and assessed frequently to determine what additional needs they may need to achieve mastery. Once they master the concept, they return to tier 1 and the regular classroom.

Tier 3 is much more intensive. It is usually a one-on-one situation or individualized to the student's learning needs. The hope is that with the additional attention and instruction, with frequent assessment, the students will be able to return to the classroom once the skill set is attained. Tier 3 documentation is also a part of the process of identifying children with specific learning disabilities. However, just because a student is in tier 3, that does not mean it will serve as a gateway to special-education identification. Special education is no longer a place; rather, it is a service to assist struggling students in the mainstream of education (Burns 2008).

Response to intervention is a type of hierarchy-treatment plan to assist struggling students. Best practice in RTI is an open-door concept with students going up and down through the tiers as is necessary to learn or master a concept or skill set they may be struggling with. It is not to be a prerequisite for special-education identification.

There are limited resources for RTI strategies in secondary education. There are a number of reasons for this lack of resources. Many do not want to struggle with the schedule concerns and content-compliance issues for graduation. Academic deficits may be already ingrained within students by the time they reach high school, and to fill those gaps while still meeting graduation requirements is very difficult. Adolescents may have struggled through school for a long time and be turned off by education because it has been difficult for them to be successful. This may manifest itself in attention difficulties or behaviors to get out of the uncomfortable situation (Fuchs, Fuchs, and Compton 2010).

Elementary RTI teams seem to be more successful in intervening in the learning process, as the students have not built up an emotional block to learning, and many of the accommodations and classroom modifications in tier 1 become more prevention than intervention focused. Elementary schools can also control some of their time better than high schools with preset bell schedules (Fuchs, Fuchs, and Compton 2010).

Response to intervention at tier 2 and tier 3 also becomes a numbers game at the secondary level. At the elementary level, there are not as many sections of each grade level as there are departmentalized classes at the high school. This means that RTI group sizes are much larger at the high school than at the elementary school, so students do not get the attention and focus at the secondary level that they do at the elementary level (Sanaosti et al. 2010). This is why primary intense intervention at the elementary level is so crucial in order for students to be successful at the secondary level.

At the secondary level, the focus needs to be on literacy in reading, writing, and mathematics. If a secondary student has not mastered these concepts, all other content-area classes will be a constant struggle, and overall failure will be inevitable. Unless a secondary school implements RTI, the failure rate will continue to grow, and the graduation rate will continue to decline.

Adolescents require different interventions from elementary students, even if the learning deficit is similar in concept. Secondary students who display severe discrepancy in literacy need to be placed in the most intensive remediation available in the school. There are a number of evidence-based reading programs for students with reading disabilities that can be modified to meet the needs of an unidentified tier 3 special-needs student (Ehren 2010).

Secondary education will see a gradual change in the quantity of RTI strategies and interventions offered in high schools and middle schools. This can be attributed to the elementary students who have been receiving tier 2 and tier 3 interventions for years in elementary school. Those students are getting older and will need some of the same modifications and accommodations to be successful at the high-school level (Friedman 2010).

One program that was developed for secondary education involved providing a research-based strategy to a small group of students three to five times a week for twenty to forty minutes daily, depending upon the needs of the students. If the high school wanted to implement this idea, the strategy had to be research based and in a scripted format. By training monitors or paraprofessionals and giving them scripts to teach from, these students' needs could be met without adding staff to the building. These students had to be assessed regularly, and after a quarter their placement had to be analyzed in terms of the success of the intervention outcome (Friedman 2010).

Providing a double dose of a subject area is another strategy to try at the secondary level. Providing two periods of reading, one in the morning and the other in the afternoon, using a research-based, scripted strategy, may impact the decoding skills and comprehension skills of limited readers in high school (Vaughn and Fletcher 2010). The use of research-based software under the supervision of a trained staff member is another option to explore in remediating secondary students. Secondary RTI requires a district thrust and push to problem-solve with respect to the time difficulties, as well as the limited resources available, resources that are nonetheless necessary for one to be successful in the implementation of RTI at the middle-school and high-school levels.

INTEGRATING THEORY INTO PRACTICE

Response to intervention is going to be one of the more difficult but still necessary initiatives that a principal has to implement at the secondary level. There are many constructs standing in the way of the implementation of this intervention. The schedule, the staffing, and the space available are just three of the barriers to overcome. Determining the research-based program content and the benchmarking assessments is crucial in monitoring for success. RTI is not just for literacy remediation, but can also be used for behavioral interventions. The format and organization of the team and the tiered structure of RTI can be structured for both areas of need.

In most teacher contracts, duties can be assigned to teachers by the build-ing administrator. Assessing whom students tend to seek out as mentors, on their own, is a good indication of who might be a strong mentor for students who might be struggling behaviorally. Utilizing the RTI structure, have a list of mentors available, so that you and the established RTI team can connect at-risk students with an adult in the building who can mentor, and model behavior for, students who are struggling behaviorally. Participating as a member of the RTI team can also be a duty assigned to staff members.

In your first year as principal, it may be difficult to have a full RTI team established if there is not one already present in the building. Some buildings are still using the intervention-assistant-team concept to intervene with chil-dren who are having difficulties. Use of a preestablished IAT team, if avail-able, can be regenerated into the establishment of a structured RTI support team. You can begin to research current RTI authors who have found success at the secondary level. You could be a trendsetter in this area.

As mentioned earlier, one of the strategies that could possibly be imple-mented in your first year is double dosing students in reading. Students could take the same class twice in one day, with different interventions. Analyze how your reading class is structured and what training might be necessary for your reading instructors. Many high-school reading classes read lower-level novels and work on comprehension. Decoding in reading may need to be the priority in these classes, and class size may be a problem. Check out the use of your paraprofessionals or monitors, and see how you can rearrange duties to provide more intervention.

Look at your beginning algebra classes. Have the instructors benchmark these students as to number sense and order of operations. This may be a good indicator of a need for remediation in the math areas before failures begin to crop up on the transcripts. Working through the junior-high or middle-school administration to gather previous data on these struggling stu-dents may give indications as to where the missing chunks of information are, so remediation can be put into play immediately. Hand-scheduling some students may provide opportunities that had not been considered by the com-puter for these at-risk students. Have counselors review the at-risk-student cumulative files to gather more information regarding previous interventions and how the strategies worked for these students.

Have your assistant principal look at the duty assignments of teachers and determine if there is a different way to schedule these people so that they are intervening with at-risk students rather than maintaining order in the lunch room or a study hall. Look at how algebra is offered second semester. If students fail semester 1, what do they do second semester? Offer semester 1 algebra second semester so there is no interruption of services for these at-risk students. Check with the district level to see if second-semester algebra could be offered in the summer for these students, to get them back on track in the math area.

Look at the failure lists midquarter. If you have students failing first quarter, is there any way you can offer those students a double dose of that subject during their day, to assist in their understanding? Maybe a monitor or paraprofessional can help by working in that classroom one period. How many co-taught classes are being offered in your school, with both a general-education teacher and a special-education teacher? Some of the at-risk students could be part of such a class, if the special-needs population is not too large in that section. To be effective in RTI, the principal and the RTI team must begin to think outside of the box. There are many constraints at the secondary level, but use your team, your focus groups, and your staff to generate ideas to meet the needs of these learners.

CASE STUDIES

- During an observation of a co-taught math class in your building, you notice that the special educator is sitting in the back of the room and is not an active part of the classroom lesson. This appears to be going on the entire period. In other co-taught classrooms you have observed, there is a give and take in instruction between the teachers. You speak to the special-needs teacher at the end of the period after she leaves, and you are informed that this is all she has been allowed to do in this class. *How do you handle this situation and make the necessary instructional changes?*
- The freshman class appears to be doing poorly in content-area subjects. The content-area teachers report that they seem lower functioning than other classes they have had in the past. Not only do the grades show a problem, but according to the teachers the content is not being covered in the timeframe that is necessary to meet the standards. The teachers complain that they have to go back to basics to get students to grasp the material. *How do you use your RTI team effectively, and how do you measure effectively what is happening in these classes?*
- The assistant principal comes to you to share that he has about five students across all grade levels who are being removed from different classes two to three times a week because of behavior. The students' grades are poor, and there have been numerous contacts with their parents. *It is now your responsibility to help strategize a solution or solutions for your assistant. What do you do?*

CHAPTER REFLECTIONS

- Response to intervention is a difficult concept to implement at the secondary level. The numbers of students assigned to teachers are very large. The rigor of the core curriculum has filled teachers' plates with a set of demands that do not include remediation. Money is scarce nationally, and in most cases additional staffing midyear is unheard of in your district, so you must think out of the box on how to utilize your staff more effectively to meet the needs of these learners. As the building leader, you must be the voice of these students. No one else speaks for them.
- Research best practice in secondary RTI. The reference page at the end of this chapter is a good place to start looking up authors. There has not been much information published about secondary RTI. Examine what your reading teacher is using for placement in the reading class, and contact the middle-school or junior-high feeders that feed students into your school to find out how students are recommended for placement in reading at the high-school level. Does the junior high have any standardized-research-assessment tool that it has been using that is effective in diagnosing specific problems in reading?
- Meet with your RTI or IAT team to brainstorm some remedies to the problems you are experiencing with students who have reading difficulties. Involve the reading teacher in this discussion. Invite a junior-high reading teacher to participate also, so that you have more than one expert in the group. Brainstorm solutions or possibilities. This is going to be ongoing for you, as long as you are the principal. Once you have figured out a solution to one learning problem, another learning issue will arise and you will be back to square one. Stay current in the research, and keep your response-to-intervention team alive and functioning effectively.

REFERENCES

Canter, A., M. Klotz, and K. Cowan. 2008. "Response to Intervention: The Future of Secondary Schools." *Principal Leadership*, February, 12–15.

Ehren, B. 2010. "Use of RTI with Older Students." *Reading Today*, August–September.

Fuchs, L., D. Fuchs, and D. Compton. 2010. "Rethinking Response to Intervention at Middle and High School." *National Association of School Psychologists*, 22–27.

Chapter Nine

Safety

THEORY

There are many facets to school safety. There is the plan that schools utilize when there is a weather emergency, or if an evacuation is needed, or if a school needs to go into lockdown because of an intruder. There is also the idea of personal safety and having a bully-free school. Bullying can have physical, verbal, and cyber aspects, from the identification of someone who is being bullied, to being a bystander, to an individual's being the person who is doing the bullying. All of these areas also tie in to school climate, which manifests itself in the students' and teachers' perceptions of how safe they feel attending school (Preble and Taylor 2009).

School climate has been defined as what happens when the adults are not present. Staffs are preoccupied with test scores and teaching and learning, but school safety has to fit into the picture also. If students do not feel safe they cannot learn. To feel safe is a physical need and a right of all human beings. The difficulty comes when trying to measure that feeling or climate. Many adults suffer from cognitive dissonance when they realize that their perception of the school climate does not match the survey data of the students (Preble and Taylor 2009).

School policy and guidelines regarding harassment and bullying are a great place to begin in assessing how ready the school is to survey the student body as to how they feel about their school climate. There are numerous surveys available to rate and describe the climate in a school building. One survey measures the interpersonal relationships within a building, by exploring things such as the number of fights taking place within the building, how teachers display that they care, and the use of teachers as role models who do not bully children (DeRosier and Newcity 2005).

Another study was completed linking character traits of students and adults at school to positive social relations at school. These traits manifest themselves as either lower antisocial behavior or greater school safety. The intervention for the antisocial behavior is dependent upon the adult intervention when dealing with that behavior. The promptness of action and the consequences of the action played into the perceptions of safe schools in this example (DeRosier and Newcity 2005).

A principal balances assuring the public that the school is safe and dealing with the problem of limited funding for providing additional resources and programs to keep the school safe. Some characteristics of a safe school include locked exterior doors, lighted stairwells, monitored hallways, and visitor identification (Paine and Cowan 2009). Nontangible characteristics might include a warm, nurturing, and welcoming environment: positive behavior and appropriate discipline for those who misbehave; positive support of student mental-health needs; regular review of safety plans; and appropriate building security, which might include a resource officer or a parking-lot attendant who monitors the comings and goings outside of the building. Last, but most important, is continuing to strengthen the connection between home and school (Preble and Taylor 2009).

If a school-climate survey has been made available to a school and it has been completed by the students and the faculty, that data can be utilized to justify a bully-prevention program within the schools. One of the most researched programs is the Olweus (2006) Bully Prevention Program, which has been around since the 1980s. It is an expensive endeavor to train a staff, but the program includes ensuring that the person being bullied is safe; that the bystander does not participate and stands up for the person being bullied; and, finally, that the person doing the bullying is stopped and immediate consequences are given, including involving the student's parents. This program enables the student body to stand firm against bullying.

As a faculty member or an administrator it is very easy to assume that the building is a safe environment for all faculty and students alike. Without taking a survey or looking at data, this is a very dangerous assumption. Safety always has to come first.

INTEGRATING THEORY INTO PRACTICE

As a new principal, review the safety plan for your building. There should be a plan for inclement weather or tornadoes. There should be a plan for a scenario where there is a bomb threat within the school, or within the stadium or gymnasium when there are events taking place, specifying the action that should transpire once a threat has been made. There should be an evacuation plan, including two different locations for students and teachers to be evacuated to, depending upon the weather and the severity of the threat. Transportation should be tied in to that plan.

There should also be a plan for a lockdown in case an intruder comes into the school, or in case of a threat from a student who is not mentally capable of making safe decisions for him- or herself or others within the building. Consider those unusual cases of special periods or different schedules because of assemblies or late starts, and whether the safety plan might look different under those situations. Supervision does not end at the bell, and staff members need to be responsible until they are told otherwise by the administration. Everyone will look toward the leader of the building for direction in these situations.

The safety plan, or an element of it, should be reviewed monthly with everyone in the building. It should be required that every person be accounted for during an emergency or an evacuation, to ensure the safety of everyone. If the whereabouts of every person on campus is not known, someone could risk a life looking for a person who may not have attended on that day. A system must be in place to account for everyone on campus. In large buildings, class lists can be placed in containers in classrooms, including every person who will be in that room during a given day. Those forms could be used for attendance purposes. The only draw back is the class lists will need to be updated as they are used, or as schedules change.

On opening day for teachers, the principal should review the safety plans and give all staff members copies. On the opening day for students, walk through the plans with everyone in the building. Take the time on day one to ensure that everyone is clear about what needs to happen with each plan. Often staff will complain because you are taking away from class time; however, the safety of everyone in the building should be paramount in everyone's mind.

If it is possible to obtain or purchase a school-climate survey, by all means attempt to have it completed. The data will be very helpful for you in establishing a baseline of concern for the climate of the building. The Olweus (2006) Bully Prevention Program has an annual survey to depict improvements and declines in the safety of the school. There are many training programs for safe schools. If you decide to select a program, ensure that there is a way to collect and measure data on an annual basis to determine the successes and failures of the school climate and how safe the stakeholders all feel within your building.

Most states now require all schools to have a bullying or harassment policy, with guidelines approved by the board of education. Someone in the district, as well as someone in your building, should be monitoring the frequency and location of the incidents to determine what patterns are being developed. The assistant principal or whoever tracks discipline should also be sharing quarterly statistics of the disciplinary referrals, the location of the behaviors, and the number of repeat offenders with all staff members. This will create a sense of urgency, as this information shows where some of the unsupervised, unsafe areas of the building seem to be in that year. Those locations could change annually, depending upon the student body and the amount of supervision in that area.

Prevention should be the key to safety. Requiring teachers to have a presence in the hallways during class changes will decrease the amount of bullying in the school. Train staff on what bullying looks like, including the subtle eye rolls, forms of exclusion, and cyberbullying that take place right before the instructor's eyes without his or her even being aware that they are taking place. If everyone in the building takes bullying seriously, the behavior should decrease. Many times a teacher will get engrossed in a discussion with someone in the classroom during a class change. It is imperative, as the leader, to stress the importance of a staff member's presence in the hallway and on the stairs. Do not forget to utilize the monitors and paraprofessionals, as well as the custodians, during these class-change times also. The presence of an adult who has been trained in aspects of bullying can make a big difference in the safety of your building, and in the lives of your children and faculty members.

CASE STUDIES

- Two students come down to the office to meet with you between classes. Your door is open, and you invite them in to talk with you. The one student is crying. When you begin to investigate, the student who is not crying, but who has come to provide moral support, explains that there is a teacher who has been bullying students, including the girl crying in your office. This is not the first time you have heard about this teacher, but you have not witnessed it, and you repeatedly hear it just from students. *Do you need to intervene in this case? Why does the teacher contract come into play in this incident? Should you check the student file? How do you resolve this particular issue?*
- A teacher is very upset because a student told him that another student has established a Web page at home that demeans this teacher. He or she wants action now. *What do you do?*
- One of the male students in your school is wearing a black trench coat that many of the faculty believe is reminiscent of several school-shooting events. The staff is upset about this student's attire. You know the student; he is really harmless, and he is not violating the school dress code. *What do you do?*

CHAPTER REFLECTIONS

- Safety is a primary responsibility of the principal. Take some time and review the plan. Take the plan and introduce yourself to the police- and fire-department officials, and make sure they have copies of the plan and are familiar with what transpires during a bomb threat, an evacuation, and a lockdown. Make sure all entrances are numbered and labeled on the outside, so if outside assistance is needed you can send them to the correct entrance door to save time. Make sure your supervisor and central office also have copies.

- Research board policies and guidelines on bullying and harassment, and make sure your student handbook is aligned with board policy. In all probability it is, and the books have probably already been printed and delivered to your building. Determine how you want to review the handbook with students and staff to ensure that everyone is aware of the school rules and the consequences for behaviors. Having a link on the school Web page is a good way to have parents access this information.

- Ask your assistant or the guidance counselors what measure the school has used annually to evaluate school climate. Ask about a bully-prevention program, and past staff development in this area. That gives you an idea of where to begin training staff, and what your next step should be for school safety.

REFERENCES

DeRosier, M., and J. Newcity. 2005. "Students' Perceptions of the School Climate: Implications for School Safety." *Journal of School Violence* 4, no. 3.

Olweus, D. 2006. *Understanding Children's Worlds: Bullying at School.* Malden, MA: Blackwell.

Paine, C., and K. Cowan. 2009. "Remembering Columbine: School Safety Lessons for the Future." *Communiqué: The Newspaper of the National Association of School Psychologists* 27, no. 6.

Preble, B., and L. Taylor. 2009. "School Climate through Students' Eyes." *Educational Leadership* 66, no. 4.

Chapter Ten

Data

THEORY

Education and data have become synonymous with school reform. High-stakes testing is now driving instruction. The grades from this data given to school systems now create inferences about the leadership of the system, the leadership of the school, and the instruction that is taking place in the classroom (Voltz, Sims, and Nelson 2010). The building principal is responsible for driving that change in instructional practices within his or her building.

Some teachers now realize that data should help prioritize changes in the curriculum as well as changes in instructional practice. Curriculum is easier to change than teacher practice, as many of the instructors have been teaching the same way for years. The data from the high-stakes assessments tells the leaders and the teachers how they are performing in the school and in the classroom, but it does not inform them of what needs to change or tell them how to implement and evaluate on a local level the best practices to positively impact state scores.

A problem with high-stakes testing is it forces teachers not to change their practice, but rather to aim their focus on the students who are not doing well, and ignore in some places the students who are above the state cut-point on the assessment (Barton and Coley 2008). Teachers need to give all students multiple opportunities to engage in constructive learning strategies that will create critical-thinking and problem-solving skills and make them active learners (Hattie 2009).

As the principal of a building, your focus regarding instruction should be assuring that authentic teaching and learning are happening in the classroom. The leadership team of the building needs to be looking at classroom assessment, individual teachers' target learning goals, and what types of feedback are utilized to determine if the students in the classroom have met those goals and objectives. Too often the results of high-stakes testing do not transfer into daily practice in the classroom. There appears to be a gap between test-preparation classes right before a high-stakes assessment and the day-to-day lesson planning and instruction within the four walls of the classroom (Schmoker 2009).

This lack of instructional connection between best practices in teaching and measurement of those practices with appropriate daily feedback appears to be where the teacher-learning gap is, undetected by the leaders of the building (Ginsberg and Brown 2009). If viable instructional formative-assessment feedback from students is not used to impact and change the instructor's teaching practice, schools will remain at the status quo.

This change is a cultural metamorphosis in the practice of teaching and learning. Teachers have to be able to accept constructive criticism, and the principal needs to be able to provide constructive suggestions and examples to assist the teacher in looking at student feedback and how it needs to influence daily instructional practices. These constructive suggestions need to provide reflection opportunities for the teacher in reviewing target learning goals and the measures that are being used to determine if those goals have been reached (Ginsberg and Brown 2009). Teaching to the test removes the richness of higher-level thinking and learning in the classroom.

The building leader needs to engage the faculty in professional learning and constructive conversations in the areas of common assessments and how the feedback gleaned from those assessments affects their daily teaching practice. Teaching needs to be proactive, and not a reaction to poor test results. Formative assessments need to be used daily to ensure that learning targets have been met, and teaching practices changed based upon that feedback. The faculty must be on the same page with these conversations, and the daily usage of evidence-based best practice. Collaboration and positive change in teaching practice determine the success of the principal as an instructional leader, and the success of student learning and critical-thinking skills.

INTEGRATING THEORY INTO PRACTICE

As a building principal you will have access to data daily. The amount of data is not the issue; it is what you do with that information, and how that information transfers into improving the teaching practice in your building, that is most important. *Meta-analysis* is a popular word today to describe the different techniques used to quantify research from the data that crosses your desk daily. It is a question of sifting through all of the information and using and applying what is important to you and your building. It will probably take professional development on your part to sort and use the information wisely.

Sorting through this data will take time, and you will need assistance initially in determining which data is the most essential and usable for beginning your work to impact instructional practice. Begin with your department chairs. The department-chair position usually has time built into the weekly schedule or has a supplemental contract to allow time for the chair's responsibilities. Check the teaching contract to see what the responsibilities are for the position and how the chairs can assist you in sorting and using the data.

As the leader, you need to create a sense of urgency as to why the data is important to the success of the school. Once you achieve buy-in from the chairs, begin to develop, with their assistance, a sense of what information should be shared initially with staff members, and how. Staff development is crucial here for the department chairs before moving forward. Your goal should be for the department chairs to become coaches within their own departments, assisting staff members in learning how to apply the data to their teaching practice. You may want to assign a math teacher who is "user friendly" to staff the duty of assisting you in sorting through all of the data. You do not have the time to do this by yourself. Remember, as a leader you need to facilitate, not micromanage.

Hopefully most of the staff members respect and listen to their department chairs. Often department-chair meetings tend to be about what supplies are needed and do not focus on the instruction or common assessments that are used within the department. Using the department chair as a coach may be a change in culture for the building. Some teachers may look at it as punitive—as an indication that you do not think they are doing their jobs, and you are using union members to administer or change their practice. This is not the philosophy you want, so buy-in is essential before beginning any initiative in your building.

Begin with a common read about professional learning communities, and follow that up with a hands-on approach during some staff meeting, to see if you can spark an interest. It may only begin with a few teachers, but that is a starting place. You will have already started focus groups, so that may be a back-door approach to getting the coaching and the data analysis started. Another strategy may be to have a brown-bag-lunch discussion group to introduce the topic over the lunch hour. Teachers bring their own lunches, and you provide dessert and give an overview of the concept. Teachers who are interested attend, and they may be your catalysts for starting the initiative.

The staff, on the whole, is aware of the consequences for the high-stakes testing within the district and/or the state. The problem is that staff members want to teach to the test a month or two in advance of the assessment, and continue business as usual the rest of the year. This reactive treatment will not bring the scores up, nor will it improve the quality of teaching in your building. Staff members must begin to understand that how they teach, and how they determine if the students are learning, is essential in impacting your building scores, and changing the culture of teaching and learning in your building. If scores of the high-stakes testing in your building are already good, having them change their practice may be more difficult, as going from good to great is difficult.

Begin with looking at the assessments that the instructors are using to determine competency in their classrooms. If two teachers are teaching different sections of the same class, are they using the same assessment to measure understanding and progress? Are your teachers aware of what formative assessment is, and how important it is in impacting learning and teaching practice? Are the only assessments that your teachers are using summative in nature, and are they using grades they created as a guide to understanding, rather than student understanding of concepts as they are presented?

These questions just begin to touch the tip of the iceberg in teaching practice. Using data as a resource to determine how instructors should teach, and how that feedback should influence their daily instruction, is something that all teachers should understand, but many just don't make the connection that grades are not the only reflection of student mastery, or a reliable one.

The use of student feedback as a means to develop change in practice is a difficult concept to get staff buy-in on, especially coming from a new principal, if staff does not recognize the problem. If you can engage your department chairs in this idea, or as you observe if you begin this discussion of formative assessment with the teacher you have watched, you may be able to divide and conquer and eventually get buy-in for this concept. Base the building budget and all purchases on the learning goals and data. Hopefully this becomes a district focus and not just a building initiative. However, before you begin any push for a new practice, make sure you have the research or evidence in hand to share and back up your premise for change.

CASE STUDIES

- As you make your first observation of a veteran teacher, you notice some problems in terms of the passive receiving of instruction. Students are not participants in the lesson, but rather unengaged, passive note takers, as the instructor continues to pontificate through the entire period. When you meet with the instructor and you suggest some changes in practice, he or she immediately accuses you of violating his or her academic freedom. *How do you respond to this accusation and instill change in the teacher's practice?*

- For the first all-day in-service for staff, you have arranged a training session on understanding and interpreting data, with a speaker and hands-on activities analyzing the school's test results. The physical-education teacher, health teacher, art teacher, and music teachers do not want to attend, as they feel that they have no impact on the tests or the scores the students achieve and want to work in their rooms on projects. *How do you respond?*
- The results from the state tests come into the hands of the teachers. Many of the students on individualized education programs did not make adequate yearly progress on the results. Teachers begin to blame the special-education teachers and their students for the poor results. You have been trying to promote co-teaching and full inclusion since you arrived at the school. The non-special-education teachers want to take no responsibility for the low scores. *What do you do to engage all of the staff and implement positive change for children on IEPs?*

CHAPTER REFLECTIONS

- Data is available to principals daily. It is how that data is aggregated, to allow staff to understand the information and use it effectively, that will impact their teaching and what is important in the overall analysis.
- The term *meta-analysis* was coined in the 1970s. It has just reached K–12 educators as accountability has become so important in education. Everything from ACT scores to AP scores cross a principal's desk annually. Too often that information is just put to the side, as educators do not know how to connect that data with classroom instruction. Having a math person available to help sort through the statistics as an extra duty, or using your department chairs as coaches, can be ways to utilize that information and dramatically change teacher practice in your building. It takes trust and time to make the change.
- Data is everyone's business and concern. Whether someone teaches physical education or is the athletic director, the entire staff, all stakeholders, need to be involved in analyzing the information and determining how it can impact assessment and teaching within the building.

REFERENCES

Barton, P., and R. Coley. 2009. "Measuring the Achievement Elephant." *Educational Leadership* 66, no. 4.

Ginsberg, M., and C. Brown. 2009. "A Day's Worth of Data." *Educational Leadership* 66, no. 4.

Hattie, J. 2009. *Visible Learning: A Synthesis of over 800 Meta-Analyses Relating to Achievement.* New York: Routledge.

Schmoker, M. 2009. "Measuring What Matters." *Educational Leadership* 66, no. 4.

Voltz, D., M. Sims, and B. Nelson. 2010. *Connecting Teachers, Students, and Standards.* Alexandria, VA: ASCD.

Chapter Eleven

Professional Learning Communities

THEORY

Constructivism is a hands-on approach to learning that is developmentally appropriate for all learners. Professional learning communities offer that same venue, but to teacher learners. Principals need to facilitate and develop the lens for teachers to look at their work, share their work, and develop the capacity to communicate with one another through a common vision (Lunenburg 2010).

One of the difficulties a principal has in promoting learning communities is the isolation of teachers within the building, within the department, and within the classroom. This isolation is one of the primary obstacles in school improvement. High-quality, effective professional development is grounded in research; inquiry; and staff participation that creates ownership and an internalization of values, and of the knowledge gleaned from honest, open communication regarding the application of the research (Jacobs and Yendol-Hoppey 2010). Professional learning communities are the vehicle for that high-quality staff development.

Professional learning communities, sometimes called "critical friends," have been around since the 1970s as a methodology to elicit positive change, improve professional skills, and raise standards (Baskerville and Goldblatt 2009). A *critical friend*, or a member of a *professional learning community*, is someone who can be trusted to look at the work of another without bias; someone who can observe, reflect upon the given data, and be part of a team that solves problems, in order to improve the initial work and raise the standards, by looking through a different pair of lenses.

This sounds easy until it is implemented. Partnering with another peer creates a vulnerability that many are uncomfortable admitting. This creates hesitancy and sensitivity for those attempting to implement a learning community. The staff members may be very guarded as far as sharing their work or any concerns that affect their profession. Sometimes a professional read on a topical subject is a good starting place to facilitate discussion. Each learning group should be no larger than eight to ten professionals.

To keep a group focused, certain values or rules need to be established as a group to facilitate discussion and create a safe environment in which to share. Some of those rules or values might include starting and ending on time; respect for all voices within the group; confidentiality outside of the group; listening to and reflecting on all comments or concerns shared; and no put-downs, even if a disagreement occurs (Hargreaves and Fullan 1998).

Every group must hold shared values, have the same mission and vision, be action and result oriented, and have a commitment to continuous improvement. The leader of each group should be more of a facilitator, timekeeper, and coach. The coach keeps the comments on topic, gives the group a reminder if someone is monopolizing the conversation, and ensures that everyone has a voice. The coach directs and facilitates the group from just discussion to action and results (Hargreaves and Fullan 1998).

Learning communities must meet on a regular basis for at least twenty to thirty minutes of uninterrupted time. The communities must look at critical topics and current research and data, and focus on students or student work. The outcomes of the work should impact the school community. Change and transformation within a community of learners never happens in isolation, but only if there is teacher discourse about those changes (Jacobs and Yendol-Hoppey 2010). Professional learning communities will lead to that transformation, as there will be joint ownership with all stakeholders based upon strong research and strong conversations toward a common mission and vision.

It may be easier for you to start with reading and sharing research. That will take away the vulnerability of sharing personal work or personal views. The principal should attempt to find time for the groups to meet during the school day, or using staff meeting time. Members of each group should be able to select the topics that interest them from the topics that are presented by the principal. The principal should also provide the first two or three research articles for each topic, to help get the group started.

There are different protocols available to read research in a timely manner and not get bogged down with the vocabulary and the length of the articles. Learning communities that have proved successful have similar traits. These communities break down teacher isolation, enhance personal and professional relationships within a building, teach and learn leadership skills by learning best practice through grounded research, free participants to give their opinions and comments to others, and initiate change in their own buildings (Kabes, Lamb, and Engstrom 2010).

The groups read research; analyze data, whether it be student or classroom data; brainstorm possible solutions; and reflect and problem-solve (Thessin and Starr 2011). Celebrating those small successes encourages the continuation of group work. Learning communities allow new ideas to be shared by stakeholders who normally do not share and competencies to be developed by a group, while initiating positive change (Pella 2011).

As a new principal in a climate of severe, mandatory educational change, it is imperative that you realize that the greatest assets the district or the building has are the staff members within them, while remembering that "school improvement" can be translated into people and practice improvement. Staff development is the key to that improvement. It is better to have the stakeholders deliver that development once parameters have been established, so that there is ownership and collegiality in initiating those improvements.

Instructors who become teacher leaders through being empowered by their principals by means of professional learning communities have a sense of contributing to change, feeling like viable members of a group rather than feeling isolated, and learning new best practices that can carry over into their individual classrooms (Barth 2001). For a principal, letting go and trusting the group is the most difficult part of the process. However, if teachers feel that they can contribute and help control the shaping of curriculum, the standards for student behavior, and the design of staff development and training, there will be a renewed sense of ownership and a true sense of positive school climate, which will trickle down into the classroom and the school.

INTEGRATING THEORY INTO PRACTICE

Using data and topics that are teacher driven is a starting place for professional learning communities. Focus groups looking at problems or data are the initiation of learning communities. As a new principal, start with focus groups, as they may sound less threatening to the staff. You present the topics from the information that you solicited at the beginning of the school year. You provide the research to get each group started, and allow staff members to join the groups that interest them, as you will get a better bang for your buck. Have the teachers complete a survey to pick a first, second, and third choice of topic. This will save time once the groups get together, as they will already be assigned and it will limit conversation that is not meaningful to solving the issues.

If you have not already done so, train your department heads or specific leaders (who may or may not have position) to become advocates and coaches for the groups. Allow them also to select the topics or problems that interest them, as it will be more beneficial to have their ownership. Ensure that the coaches are comfortable with their new role before breaking into formal groups. Sometimes a demonstration of volunteers can illustrate or role-play what a focus group looks like in practice, which may alleviate some of the anxiety. Establishing group norms will be critical if staff is not used to this type of group work.

Learning communities and/or focus groups should start on topics that have meaning to them and are nonthreatening to personal practice. Once a group gets comfortable with and proficient at reading the research and reflecting on and problem-solving the issues, then the proponents for change can begin to expand their repertoire. Looking at issues within a building is nonthreatening because it does not affect a person personally.

Another method of expanding where the group grows and goes to is looking at student work and evaluating the level of learning that is demonstrated on the worksheets and/or the tests, which will give you some indication of what is happening in the classroom when you are not present. This is not an evaluation issue for you to handle, but rather a teacher growth issue, to be initiated and conducted among peers. This represents an evolution of trust that must transpire within each of the learning communities. Building on this trust, teachers can look at common assessments and what, as a group, they want the learning level to reflect. This has also evolved into peers discussing behavior problems with one another, peer observations and discussions, and school-improvement initiatives. Teachers can be members of different groups at the same time. The issue is that you, as the principal, need to make the time available. Many schools have late starts or early dismissals, which is a wonderful vehicle for working through issues in learning communities.

From the start of these focus groups make it clear that they must be action oriented, with a solution or recommendation to staff provided by the end of the semester or year, depending upon what you set as a timeline. There should be a note taker on each team who summarizes what is transpiring at each meeting, so that the staff is aware of the progress and there are no surprises at the end of the timeline. A blog is a wonderful tool for this sharing, as comments can be added and factored into the problem solving at each subsequent meeting. For you to let go of all the problems, which can be extremely difficult, and allow staff to contribute will facilitate faster change, and the building vision and goals can be reached sooner. It is a win-win for everyone. Remember, you set the stage and organize the actors to facilitate change for students and teachers toward best practice.

CASE STUDIES

- The focus groups are established from the initial goal setting developed at the beginning of the school year. The groups are in full discussion after reading the research that you presented on each topic to each group. When the minutes are posted on the blog as to where the groups are going, you are surprised by and worried about the direction and some of the radical solutions that seem to be developing within a couple of groups. *What can you do to refocus or redirect the group?*
- Your learning communities have evolved to the point where you suggest that a parent be added to the mix to help problem-solve some community issue in regard to which the staff feels that there may be a solution that helps involve more parents. You select the parent based upon the confidence level of the parent, someone who you know will give an honest appraisal and opinion, without intimidation. As you walk by the different groups, you overhear what sounds like an argument between a very involved parent and a very opinionated teacher who is very active in the union. The argument appears to be getting out of control, and the coach and the other members are in awe as they watch the situation deteriorate. *What do you do?*
- As an introduction to focus groups you recruit some young teachers who want to be involved, to role-play a focus group looking at student work. These teachers are viewed as rookies by some of the veterans. You realize it takes self-confidence on the part of the teachers to role-play in front of their large peer group, as many in the large group may not recognize the teachers' role-playing because many of the veterans stay within their own rooms or departments. As the example transpires, some of the veteran staff members make loud side comments that interrupt the group, which causes some laughter and thus undermines the seriousness of the role-play to the point that the teachers in the group forget the direction of the example being illustrated. *What can you do, as the leader, to squelch the laughter, and save the demonstration so that others will buy into the initiative?*

CHAPTER REFLECTIONS

- Professional learning communities (synonymous with *focus groups*) are productive, professionally stimulating, and effective for impacting school change.
- Learning communities are a form of constructivism, as the members have a hands-on approach to problem solving.
- The principal can control the group makeup and the research by having teachers sign up for a first, second, and third choice of topics. Topics should be based upon data such as discipline records over the past few years or test scores: something that can be owned by staff members.
- Select coaches for each group based upon position or natural leadership within the building. All coaches should be trained prior to instituting the entire staff in the process. This could be accomplished before school begins, after you have spoken to and gathered information from all staff members to determine the informal leadership of the staff.
- If at all possible, break up departments within the groups to prevent side conversations and generate some more creative solutions.
- Once the topics have been decided, you and the assistant principal should determine what research should be shared with each group. This is the starting place for every group, and involves the assistant in a different leadership role.
- As a principal or an assistant principal, find a group of other building administrators outside the district and cultivate relationships with them so that you can develop your own learning community for issues that surround building administrators.

REFERENCES

Baskerville, D., and H. Goldblatt. 2009. "Learning to Be a Critical Friend: From Professional Indifference through Challenge to Unguarded Conversations." *Cambridge Journal of Education* 39, no. 2, 205–21.

Hargreaves, A., and M. Fullan. 1998. *What's Worth Fighting For Out There*. New York: Teachers College Press.

Jacobs, J., and D. Yendol-Hoppey. 2010. "Supervisor Training within a Professional Learning Community." *Teacher Education Quarterly*, Spring.

Kabes, S., D. Lamb, and J. Engstrom. 2010. "Graduate Learning Communities: Transforming Educators." *Journal of College Teaching and Learning* 7, no. 5.

Lunenburg, F. 2010. "Creating a Professional Learning Community." *National Forum of Educational Administration and Supervision Journal* 27, no. 4.

Pella, S. 2011. "A Situative Perspective on Developing Writing Pedagogy in a Teacher Professional Learning Community." *Teacher Education Quarterly*, Winter.

Thessin, R., and J. Starr. 2011. "Supporting the Growth of Effective Professional Learning Communities Districtwide." *Kappan Magazine* 92, no. 6.

Chapter Twelve

Ethical Decision Making

THEORY

Ethics has been called the philosophy of morals (Callahan 1988). Morality is a learned behavior. It can be broken down into many facets, two of which are relationships and caring. A person can care about another person without establishing a formal relationship with that person. According to Beck (1994), caring comprises three activities, which she labels as the "three Rs": *receiving*, *responding*, and *remaining*. To receive, one must be open to others. To respond, one must be willing to accept another. To remain, one must keep the relationship going. An educational leader needs to portray that caring behavior within and outside the school setting.

There are times when a leader must accept the common good within everyone in his or her organization (Callahan 1988). In this particular scenario, serving the common good means creating an atmosphere or culture such that students feel comfortable in giving their views on school problems and possible solutions to those problems. This means of increasing student voice has been shown to help reengage alienated students by providing them a stronger sense of ownership in their schools. When individuals have a sense of control over their environment, they will feel more intrinsically motivated to participate and contribute in a positive manner (Johnson 1991). Participation and being listened to constitutes the beginning of a relationship, which ultimately opens the doors to responding and remaining behaviors among all constituents within a building.

Caring is a process. It can be characterized as an attitude of making oneself available to another (Blackham 1959). It does not have to be a discussion about love, but instead it can be a relatedness of a person to the world as a whole, not just to an individual (Fromm 1956). As a person becomes aware of, knowledgeable about, or understanding of another's reality or point of view, a feeling of community should develop, and the process will and can be received by another person.

Through this openness, both responsibility and acting responsively begin to evolve (Noddings 1984). It is through this responsiveness that genuine community develops (Gilligan 1982). As a building leader begins to recognize and acknowledge the feelings and fears of the adolescent, a type of responsibility and responsiveness begins to develop. Through this process, a sense of community and comfort evolve. Goleman (1995) points out that empathy is a fundamental attribute of emotional intelligence. Empathy established early in life will allow someone to be able to understand another's anger, and share joy and sorrow with another person. Schools need to pay more attention to emotional intelligence because it adds value to both the cognitive and affective domains.

This commitment to others creates a connection that promotes a healthy and satisfying culture (Mead 1970). A healthy culture promotes constancy and stability and will assist administrators and adolescents in making strong and successful decisions. The value of being cared about creates represents relationships. In a school, being cared about does not mean that there are no rules or structure or discipline, but rather that there are healthy relationships, and those relationships are respected and valued by all stakeholders.

Decision making is a critical aspect of a building leader's responsibility, and those daily decisions will determine the atmosphere, climate, and culture of a building. When an administrator fails to respond to a problem in a timely fashion, his or her hesitancy can be interpreted as a decision, and the wrong message may be given to the school, thus ultimately affecting the culture of the building.

All decisions need to be made in an ethical manner. A leader needs to ask the following questions: How do my relationships affect my decision? (Care) Who defines or controls my decision, and are there long-perpetuated systemic flaws that must be addressed? (Critique) How is my organization is governed, and how do I properly balance individual needs with the good of the whole organization? (Justice; Starratt 1991). This triangular process assists the leader in making clear, common-sense decisions without leaving any of the details of the problem or dilemma out of the process. Through this process, students will take a priority role in the school decision outcome (Gorman and Pauken 2003).

Schools should be safety nets for students, where adolescents may try on different hats or behaviors to determine who they are and who they want to become. The hat should be big enough so that every teen has room to fail successfully without losing dignity. It is only through this action from the administration, and its reaction to an adolescent's failure, that higher-level reasoning can be established and become a part of the student's daily decision making and childhood resilience.

This ability and persistence translates into making ethical decisions and ultimately affects the climate and culture of a building. Starratt (1991) describes the foundation of an ethical school as being composed of the daily decisions and relationships that the building leader creates. Through the decision-making process, the leader also has to allow enough room for himself or herself to evaluate the decisions that are made, and have the personal fortitude and common sense to go back and correct the injustices that might have resulted from impulsive, noncaring political decisions.

A leader should never underestimate the power of being cared about or developing healthy relationships while still maintaining consistency and safety within a building. A strong, ethical leader can manage a building while instilling the necessary ethical values and weaving them into the daily, standards-based academic pedagogy. It is through this healthy responsiveness and respect that a building culture can develop resiliency. This resiliency can create an ethically fit culture (Robbins 2007).

Decision making is not usually just a right or wrong answer. It could be a choice or a decision about similar responses giving way to different consequences (Klinker 2003). There may not be just one answer to resolve the issue (Strike and Ternasky 1993). The leader must take into account the needs of the student, putting aside personal interests, accepting the consequences of the decision, and ethically taking into account the whole caring community of learners (Robbins 2007).

Starratt (2005) developed a framework for ethical decision making and moral educational leadership, taking into account seeing both the good and bad in people and being able to forgive for the betterment of the school. As a building leader, you will make a greater impact on the school culture by looking at the common good in everyone and using that virtue as part of the decision-making process. Starratt (2005) believes that taking into account the moral responsibilities of the leader when making decisions will create a stronger sense of transformational leadership and higher ideals within the building culture.

Administrators are trained in ethics. There is a major difference between studying ethics in a classroom, and making ethical decisions and living with the consequences of those decisions (Sternberg 2011). It is imperative, when making decisions, that an administrator never lose his or her guiding compass of values when the clouds of political pressure from within or without attempt to compete with or take over the decision-making process (Burge 2009).

A building leader must consider the public interest of the building and the community when making decisions. The legal ramifications, as well as the financial obligations, are forces within the decision-making context. There is a dependency on all of the factors and forces that come into play when making an ethical decision (Cranston, Ehrich, and Kimber 2003). A leader must be empathetic and nonjudgmental when researching the issue. He or she should have a mental or physical structure in place when deliberating the possible outcomes of a problem. There is no right or wrong answer; however, the leader should always attempt to err in favor of the student, as that is why he or she became an administrator in the first place. Ethical decision-making is something that will occur in administration daily, and a leader needs to take into account his or her values and the time necessary to make a decision that will impact the betterment of the entire building.

INTEGRATING THEORY INTO PRACTICE

A school leader tends to make ethical decisions every day, and these affect and reflect the leadership style and the culture of a building. This style and culture are reflected through word of mouth, e-mails, and tweets within the community. Rendering a decision can become a political nightmare for the building leaders. Something that appears small in the entire scheme of things within the building can have devastating effects within the building, the district, and the community. It is imperative to give each issue some time, some discussion, and some value before issuing an edict.

A principal or assistant may get stopped in the hallway and asked a question that might have ramifications that the leader hasn't even thought of in giving his or her impulsive response. Having some form of communications technology or paper with you at all times will assist you in making strong, thoughtful decisions. It is very easy to respond yes or no, but it is better to respond, "Let me get back to you later." Keep in mind that "later" should not run into days at a time without any communication saying you are still wrestling with the concern and you will get back to that person by a certain date, as not making a decision is interpreted as meaning that you have already made the decision by your silence and lack of response.

Many of the difficult decisions will involve student discipline, and zero tolerance. As a problem presents itself, refer first to the district policy and/or guidelines. Often these guidelines are written very vaguely on purpose, to allow room for interpretation by the administrator in a given situation. It is not imperative that you respond immediately to a difficult situation without some type of formal investigation and discussion with the parties involved, including another administrator.

Zero tolerance is a general term that evolved because of the Columbine incident. It is not a "one size fits all" form of discipline. Keep in mind that natural consequences are the best learning experiences for an adolescent. Ask yourself, what is the purpose for the discipline that is issued? Is it merely a punitive consequence, or should there be a learning curve for the student in the process, so that the behavior is not repeated?

Discipline is established to teach, and not just to give consequences. If the consequence does not match the behavior, there is little to no learning taking place. Learning from the consequence is essential if the behavior is not to be repeated by the student. Sometimes in zero-tolerance cases, removing the student is the only response. However, keep in mind that if someone can have contact with this student—such as an outside counselor or a home tutor in a library or some other public place—during the removal period, it will ensure that the student is safe, and that no one gets hurt because there is an unsupervised student in the community during the day.

Sometimes with repeat behavioral offenders it is easy to become personally aggravated; or some other adult within the building may be at his or her limit with a particular student's behavior. In determining a decision, it is important to take a step back from the situation, and ensure that the consequence being issued is not influenced by personal agitation, or by political pressure from within the building or from a parent or community member.

Ethical decision making can be very difficult, and you may second-guess yourself in the process because of all of the political pressure falling upon you. Spend some time looking at all of the issues. Ask yourself, what is in the best interest of the adolescent? Keep in mind that adolescents still react like children because of their brain development, even though they may be larger than you. When students are asked why they did what they did, they usually respond that they do not know. In most cases this is correct, as their impulsivity gets the best of their behavior, and they really do not know why they did what they did. It just seemed right at the time to them. That is how an adolescent's mind works.

In all decision-making processes, ensure that as the leader of the building you can stand by the decision that you have made, despite all of the political fallout that may occur. If you can defend your position based upon all of the facts you investigated; and you feel the decision you made was the right thing to do for the student and the school community; and you can live with your judgment, then you made the correct decision. No decision will ever have total consensus or be popular with everyone. It is these problems and decisions that make being an administrator of a school one of the most difficult positions in a district.

On the other side of the decision-making process are the decisions you make with and about staff members. These are not easy situations either. If a problem arises, check the teacher or the staff contract first to determine the violation. If it is unclear, talk with another administrator; or, if you have a good relationship with a union representative, run some questions by the member. Be sure that you have a trust relationship with this person. You can pose your concerns in the form of questions such as, "If I did this, what would be the union's move on that response to the problem?" Having a strong, healthy relationship with staff members will help facilitate your decision-making ability. However, a union representative will always defend the actions of the other members, as that is their job. Your job is to follow the contract and ensure that all students and staff are safe, and that students are in the best-nurturing learning environment possible while attending your school.

Ethical decision-making is very difficult, as it needs to take into account how your relationships affect your decision-making ability, what flaws or past practice have dictated in this situation, and whether you have considered the needs of the individual as well as what is good for the entire organization. Contemplating these factors should give you clarity in making the right decision for everyone involved in the problem.

CASE STUDIES

- A student in the sophomore class has brought a discipline problem to your attention. A student has come to you and said that he or she has been threatened with bodily harm by another student. Your initial response is to suspend the threatening student, but that student shares with you that he or she has been teased and called harsh names by this student and others in the class. *What is the ethical thing to do to meet the needs of everyone's safety?*
- A teacher comes to you in tears, saying that a student in his or her class has posted disparaging remarks about him or her on a social-networking site. After investigating, another student gives you a printed copy of the remarks and page. When you begin the discipline process the parent objects, as the page was developed at home and not at school. To this point the page has not caused any disruption within the school, except for the teacher being very upset. *What is the ethical response, and what are the consequences?*
- A graduating senior misses graduation practice. The rule of the school is that a student cannot participate in commencement activities without attending practice. You hear from other students that the senior had been out partying with friends the night before, and had difficulty getting out of bed to attend the practice. The parents of the student explain that they never knew of this rule, and never received the written communication sent

home. Furthermore, the student was tending a sick grandparent late into the evening and overslept. The senior confirms the parents' story. The parents cannot believe that an educator would deny a student the right to walk with his or her class and receive a diploma. Board members have been contacted. There is no formal policy on this rule. It is only listed in guidelines. *What is the ethical thing to do?*

CHAPTER REFLECTIONS

- Building administrators make decisions that impact students, teachers, and the community daily. It is very important that principal impulsivity not interfere with those outcomes, so that a leader can get on with the next issue.
- Every situation and decision requires a thoughtful process. This process includes investigation, personal relationships, past practice, and balancing the individual needs of the person involved in the situation with the well-being of the organization on a whole.
- Every decision rendered by an administrator will not be popular with everyone, and consensus is difficult or nearly impossible to reach in a secondary community. It is important to weigh every decision carefully and thoughtfully so that the interests of the student, the teacher, and the school community benefit from the decision. A principal must take out his or her personal bias in rendering a decision. What is good for kids is not always popular with kids.
- Natural consequences are imperative in creating a learning experience for a student. If the consequence does not reflect the behavior learning will not occur, and the same student may repeat the behavior at a later date. For the leader of a school, teaching appropriate life consequences is as important as teaching pedagogy. Making ethical decisions and recommendations is one of the largest responsibilities of a school leader.

REFERENCES

Beck, L. 1994. *Reclaiming Educational Administration as a Caring Profession*. New York: Teachers College Press.

Blackham, J. H. 1959. *Six Essentialist Thinkers*. New York: Harper and Row.

Burge, E. 2009. "Doing 'Good Work': Negotiating Possibilities in Ethical Challenges." *New Directions for Adult and Continuing Education*, no. 123 (Fall).

Callahan, J. 1988. *Ethical Issues in Professional Life*. New York: Oxford University Press.

Cranston, N., L. Ehrich, and M. Kimber. 2003. "The 'Right' Decision? Towards an Understanding of Ethical Dilemmas for School Leaders." *Westminster Studies in Education* 26, no. 2.

Fromm, E. 1956. *The Art of Loving*. New York: Harper and Row.

Gilligan, C. 1982. *In a Different Voice: Psychological Theory and Women's Development*. Cambridge, MA: Harvard University Press.

Goleman, D. 1995. *Emotional Intelligence*. New York: Bantam Books.

Gorman, K., and P. Pauken. 2003. "The Ethics of Zero Tolerance." *Journal of Educational Administration* 41, no. 1, 24–36.

Johnson, J. H. 1991. *Student Voice: Motivating Students through Empowerment*. Eugene: Oregon School Study Council. ERIC Document Service Reproduction no. ED 337 875.

Klinker, J. F. 2003. "An Analysis of Principals' Ethical Decision Making Using Rest's Four Component Model of Moral Behavior." Paper presented at the annual convention of the American Educational Research Association, Chicago.

Mead, M. 1970. *Culture of Commitment: A Study of the Generation Gap*. New York: Doubleday.

Noddings, N. 1984. *Caring: A Feminine Approach to Ethics and Moral Education*. Berkley: University of California Press.

Robbins, S. 2006. "Ethical Decision Making by Educational Leaders: The Need For a Cultural Multiparadigm Approach." *International Schools Journal* 26, no. 1.

Robbins, S. 2007. "Ethical Decision-Making by Educational Leaders: Its Historical Context and Useful Frameworks." *International Schools Journal* 27, no.1.

Starratt, R. 1991. "Building an Ethical School: A Theory for Practice in Educational Leadership." *Educational Administration Quarterly* 27, no. 2, 185–202.

Sternberg, R. 2011. "Ethics from Thought to Action." *Educational Leadership* 68, no. 6.

Strike, K. A., and P. L. Ternasky. 1993. *Ethics for Professionals in America: Perspectives for Preparation and Practice*. New York: Teacher College Press.

Chapter Thirteen

Reflections

THEORY

Reflection takes individual time and self-examination. It is essential to get accurate feedback through this introspection process so that a leader's personal perception is congruent with the feedback that is given. Listening to others and journaling to self also form part of the process. A school reflects the leadership of the building (Rooney 2009). A collection of artifacts or evidence is necessary to glean a true portrait of the building leadership that is reflected in the building culture, and the success story of the teaching and learning results (Goldring et al. 2009). Making a judgment on the true effectiveness of oneself as a building leader is essential for continuous school improvement (Goldring et al. 2009).

There are countless attributes and facets to the building-principal position. The difficulty that many administrators struggle with is identifying what dimensions of the position should be examined (Goldring et al. 2009). The list of attributes includes, but is not limited to, the following: instructional planning, interpersonal skills, decision-making skills, school climate, and management responsibilities for the entire facility (Williams et al. 2009). This extensive list makes it difficult to know where to begin.

Most building principals believe in retrospect that most of their day has been spent in making effective instructional decisions, and impacting adolescents. However, several studies present evidence that the bulk of the principal's day is spent in managing tasks that have little or nothing to do with teaching and learning (Williams 2001). As an administrator, it is important for you to create a practice of self-reflection and self-analysis to determine what individual strategies and skill sets you are using effectively during the bulk of each school day. If the principal is knowledgeable about what is being taught in the classroom, then the focus of this administrator should be to provide the necessary materials, technologies, and collaboration times to allow that instruction to take place (Kearney 2005).

During the practice of self-reflection, the building leader should consider to what extent the classroom instruction matches the standards. Is the building team in an organized, succinct flux of continuous improvement based upon evidence-based practice? Are new partnerships continuing to develop with parents and community members? Is the school climate a safe and nurturing environment, even when the classroom doors are closed, and teachers and staff members are not being observed (Habegger 2008)?

Principals tend to feel great stress in the age of high-stakes testing and accountability. Research suggests that positive interactions and collaboration between a principal and the teachers create a significant positive factor in the improvement process (Egley and Jones 2005). This process needs to be examined and analyzed by the leader to ensure that the process is going in his or her intended direction, and has not taken on a life of its own.

Feedback is essential in reflective practice. A different survey to teachers, parents, and graduating seniors will give the leader information that he or she may never have considered. The teachers can give input as to what they want changed, and reveal the undercurrent that might possibly be within the building, unnoticed by the leader (Cassel 2003). The parent club can sponsor a survey or a phone chain to solicit information, and compile a list of positives within the school community, as well as possible concerns. Each year's graduating seniors can give information by answering simple questions about what they found to be strengths and weaknesses in their programming, and what they perceived the overall climate of the school to be. Between all of the surveys, these themes will produce a picture for the principal to compare to his or her own perception of how the year transpired. It is with the help of this information that the principal can self-reflect as to the productivity and success of the school year that has just ended, and begin to establish some possible goals for the following school year.

Some of the theme topics might include the effectiveness of the team, and the success of the evidence-based practices implemented. The effectiveness of the handling of the discipline, and were all cases handled with student dignity in mind? Is the counseling department effective in more than just scheduling? Is there prevention as well as an intervention component to the program? Do all members of the student body, including ESL students, at-risk students, special-education students, and new transient students, feel that they are a part of the school? Are athletics and co-curricular participants, and the fans, displaying appropriate sportsmanship? These are just a few of the themes that may surface with the results of the surveys and the leader's observations (Cassel 2003).

All of these factors influence how a building principal determines the effectiveness of his or her leadership throughout the school year. There will always be weaknesses in the program, but that evidence of practice will assist the leader in setting new goals, in conjunction with all of the stakeholders, for the following school year(s).

INTEGRATING THEORY INTO PRACTICE

Reflection can be therapeutic but also very painful, as you begin to scrutinize the successes and the flaws within a school year. Attempting to reflect just in a summative format at the end of a school year can be more difficult and less effective than contemplating the positives and the negatives via a personal journal, a personal blog, or a diary as the year and the different issues progress.

With that personal year-long documentation and the positive and negative feedback that arises from the different annual surveys or evaluations from the teachers, the parents, and the students, common themes will surface and be identified in concert with your year-long perceptions. That information, in conjunction with your personal documentation, will give you direction for the following year, so that you can establish possible goals, in conjunction with staff, based upon that evidence.

Another possible technique to assist in your regular documentation throughout the year would be to develop a framework matrix listing annual goals and objectives on one axis and the months of the year on the other axis. By keeping this as a working document on your desktop, you can write notes as things happen, either at the end of a school day, or the next morning before the teachers and staff arrive. This will give you the opportunity to use the data you collect throughout the year to revise and tweak the stakeholder surveys as needed, based upon actual events. It also gives you and your fellow administrators monthly discussion topics, so you can problem-solve and be preventative in your future practice.

This documentation will also assist you in preparing for your annual review with your supervisor, as well as assist you in preparing for the evaluations you are responsible for implementing. Any type of authentic artifact that can be utilized to improve the status quo will make a positive difference within your school and program.

Self-reflection is difficult and requires you to set aside some time every day to think, and to critique how certain situations were handled, as they relate to teaching and learning, staff members, student discipline, and parents and community members. Keep in mind that everyone in your learning community, inside of the building and at events outside of the school, reflects you and your leadership style. It is for this reason that your notes and written descriptions are so crucial for real educational change and improvement.

Discipline records should be summarized quarterly and shared with staff, to determine what the pattern of repetitive behavior is and how that behavior can be managed more effectively. Without the data, you are leading blindly. This lack of information can and will negatively affect your school climate. It is also good to collect data regarding the cleaning and monitoring of the cafeteria and hallways. This allows you to discuss and prevent future problems with staff, the facility, the student body, and visitors. Developing a clear, concise framework or matrix of documentation that works for you and the other administrators will facilitate a safe, nurturing, forward-thinking learning community.

CASE STUDIES

- At your annual review with your superintendent, you are asked to listen to your evaluation and supply documentation as to how you attained your annual goals and completed your self-evaluation. This year, you did not make time to reflect, or to document, on a daily basis, incidents and/or situations that occurred throughout the school year. You attempted to self-reflect the day before the data was due. At the meeting, the superintendent asked for the artifacts, and the goals for the following school year that stemmed from the documentation you generated yesterday. *How do you develop worthwhile objectives, and/or what should you do in the future?*
- As you review the results from the surveys and your own personal data, as well as what the other administrators have shared with you at your weekly meetings, you begin to see a striking pattern of one teacher's name continuing to surface in regard to bullying students and bullying staff members. You were so busy throughout the year that you did not reflect on your own data until you read some of the surveys, which triggered your recognition of the common theme. *How do you handle this situation before the start of the next school year?*
- You review all of the surveys after graduation. You have just checked out your last staff member, and you are tired—and relieved that the year has ended without any major incident. As you begin to collect the common themes from all three surveys, you notice that the general tone appears more negative than positive from the students, the parents, and even many of the staff members. The effectiveness of your leadership style is in question, and you find yourself getting very defensive about the data, even though they are from three different sources. *What is your next move?*

CHAPTER REFLECTIONS

- Reflection is difficult for everyone. For an administrator, finding the time to self-evaluate and document can become just one more thing. Self-reflection will assist you in being a stronger and more empathetic leader. Self-reflection is a form of effective leadership.
- A principal's day goes very quickly from one activity to another. It can be very reactive, and the time may not be available daily to be the effective instructional leader that you want to be in your building. Sometimes it feels that you do not even have time to look at the data, let alone gather it, to make constructive, well-documented decisions. Finding time before you leave, after the building is quiet, or, alternatively, arriving early may be the only ways to document and evaluate your previous day. Personal documentation is extremely valuable and worthwhile for setting new, effective personal and building goals.
- Communicating the reflective information that you gather and document will provide specific, authentic discussion topics for your focus groups or learning communities to use in making effective change within the building, and assist you in growing and changing your leadership traits and style to become more effective and productive.

REFERENCES

Cassel, R. 2003. *Let Democracy Become Alive in the High Schools of America So That Seniors and Parents can Evaluate those Programs.* EBSCO Publishing.

Egley, R., and B. Jones. 2005. "Can Accountability Be Inviting? An Assessment of Administrators' Professionally and Personally Inviting Behaviors." *Journal of Invitational Theory and Practice* 2.

Goldring, E., X. Cravens, J. Murphy, A. Porter, S. Elliot, and B. Carson. 2009. "The Evaluation of Principals: What and How Do States and Urban Districts Assess Leadership?" *Elementary School Journal* 110, no.1.

Habegger, S. 2008. "The Principal's Role in Successful Schools: Creating a Positive School Culture." *Principal NASEP.*

Kearney, K. 2005. "Guiding Improvements in Principal Performance." *Leadership Association of California School Administrators.*

Rooney, J. 2009. "Who Evaluates the Principal?" *ASCD Educational Leadership.*

Williams, E., G. Persaud, and T. Turner. 2008. "Planning for Principal Evaluation: Effects on School Climate and Achievement." *Educational Planning* 17, no. 3.

Williams, H. 2001. "Teachers' Perceptions of Principal Effectiveness in Selected Secondary Schools in Tennessee." *Curriculum and Supervision, Central Washington University.*

Chapter Fourteen

Epilogue

Most chapters at the end of a textbook tend to wrap up discussions and give some direction or advice for what the reader should do in transitioning to the next phase of his or her professional life. This chapter is more of a synopsis or summary of the preceding chapters, in a step-by-step format for easy reference—a guide to the first year in a new secondary administrative position. The material is bulleted for convenience.

CHAPTER 1: WHERE DO I BEGIN?

- As you visit the building for the first time, set up meetings with the secretary and custodian to begin to get an understanding of what has occurred prior to your arrival, and to get a sense of the building from their perspective. Have an informal agenda that you keep to yourself, but take notes that you can revisit after you have collected more data.
- Share with the secretary how you would like to the have the office function, and ask for a copy of the cleaning schedule and custodial names and shifts.
- Set up a meeting with the other administrators in the building, including the athletic director. Develop an agenda, and take notes informally to get an understanding of how each person has operated, and what the individual responsibilities have looked like in the past. Keep these notes for future reference.
- Set up a meeting with the parent club presidents. It would be a good idea for them to all be present at the same time to let them get to know you, and to let you get names with faces. These are the movers and the shakers in the building, and a strong support system for you.

- Orchestrate a meeting with the department chairs or the teacher leaders. Again, have an informal agenda. This is an opportunity to learn what worked, and what the teachers liked and disliked, in the past. It is worthwhile information. Listen, and make no promises.
- Meet with the student leaders of the senior class. Ask questions from the informal agenda to determine what the climate has been like over the past three years. This is an excellent opportunity to begin to get to know the student leaders.
- Meet with other principals within the district, such as elementary principals, to get an outside perspective.
- Meet with the superintendent and review your notes with him or her, and see if they are what he or she sees at the building. Together with your administrative team, plan the opening day for staff members and the opening day for students.

CHAPTER 2: GOAL SETTING

- Meet with the entire staff, and brainstorm about the strengths and achievements of the school, and the weaknesses. Compare this information with the information you gathered at your initial meetings. Develop common themes, to lead focus groups to study the information and develop possible solutions.
- Find research that connects with the topics, so the focus groups have some evidence to base their brainstorming on.
- All staff development should be tied to those topics, so there is purpose to the training.

CHAPTER 3: THE ASSISTANT-PRINCIPAL ROLE

- The assistant principal has a difficult road to follow. In many situations, the assistant ends up with all discipline. The assistant, with the support of his or her principal, should request all classroom-management plans to review. If the plans are not written correctly or do not have realistic goals and consequences, positive or negative, meet with that teacher to rewrite the plan. Remember, the reason the plans need to be reviewed is so the assistant can support the classroom teacher in discipline.
- As an assistant, find a mentor, so there is someone who can meet and talk with you on a regular basis. There is some isolation in this position, and often not too many positive interactions.

- Meet with your principal to determine roles and communication lines. If you are the principal, meet with your veteran assistants and establish some common, consistent communication patterns and a workable chain of command.

CHAPTER 4: THE ELEMENTARY PRINCIPAL

- As the new leader in the building, it is imperative that you look at last year's student data. Research what evidence-based assessment the system uses for benchmarking, and develop a schedule utilizing all of the specialists in the building to benchmark every student the first week in school. This data will determine who needs intervention in reading and math. The intervention schedule can be developed based upon this need.
- Ensure that you have a positive-behavior support plan in place for the entire school. This culture will permeate to all who enter your building and will create a positive, safe environment for all students.
- Look at the licensure of all of your teachers to determine which ones have advanced degrees and a reading endorsement on their licenses. If the teacher is a strong person who seems to have strong relationships, talk to your curriculum director to see if he or she can have cognitive-coaching training to act as a literacy coach in your building. This will provide staff development on a daily basis for all teachers, and provide positive practice in your building.

CHAPTER 5: RELATIONSHIPS

- Relationships are the most important part of being an administrator. The first few weeks are exhausting and overwhelming for a new administrator, but this is the time to be out and about in the hallways, at events, in the lunchroom, in the parking lot at the end of the day, by the buses, and in the teacher lounge.
- Meeting with parent groups and attending booster meetings will begin to establish some firm acquaintance-type relationships that hopefully will develop into friendships that support you and your position.
- Building relationships and having an open-door policy for teachers, students, and parents will allow you to know your constituents on a first-name basis. It is essential to have a trust factor if change, reform, and school improvement are ever to ignite in your secondary school.

CHAPTER 6: COMMUNICATION

- Communication is the beginning to all relationships. Technology is a tool for writing blog bulletins, e-mailing information, and maintaining interactive Web pages, but it is not the only way to interact with all of the stakeholders. The community and the school want to get to know you as a person and a leader. Face-to-face contact is the best way to begin a trusting relationship.
- School improvements in the high-powered institutions have a strong relationship base before moving forward. Trust in a leader can make or break a reform initiative. Knowing your audience will assist in any presentation about any change proposals.
- Focus groups are a strong venue in which to promote change. As the leader, always attempt to provide peer-reviewed articles on the topic to begin discussions in the groups. Make sure departments are split up so that all parties can be heard and it will not be "business as usual." All notes from every focus-group meeting, parent meeting, and staff meeting should be posted, so that everyone knows what is happening and there are no secrets or hidden agendas, just transparency.

CHAPTER 7: TEACHING AND LEARNING

- *Teaching* and *learning* are the buzzwords that are in all of the journals. Teacher accountability and high-stakes testing are concerns for everyone. It is imperative that you and your staff begin to develop common assessments. Students should receive the same rigorous instruction, regardless of teacher style, and be assessed on that information.
- Critical thinking and problem solving should be a part of every classroom. Guidance counselors have an excellent knowledge, based upon parent requests and complaints, of classes that are not challenging or engaging. Relationships with the guidance department are essential to creating a strong learning environment.
- A common grading practice throughout the building provides a common rigor throughout all courses. High expectations and strong student engagement prepare all students for postsecondary education.

CHAPTER 8: RESPONSE TO INTERVENTION

- Response to intervention (RTI) is a tiered approach to providing additional assistance to students who are struggling in many subjects or just struggling in a specific topic or unit. Double dosing students in the content or remediating those areas where the student is struggling can not only assist students with the rigor, but also potentially bring up high-stakes-testing scores.
- Many teachers, depending upon the contract, have duty assignments. One of the duty assignments could be to help or mentor a student behaviorally, to assist that student in becoming successful. This is another technique for keeping adolescents on track toward graduation.
- Counselors offering social-skill groups to struggling students can assist academically if the student is more concerned with friendships, anger-management issues, grief, or a poor home life. RTI should be both a prevention and intervention program. Students can move up and down the hierarchy of tiers depending upon individual needs.

CHAPTER 9: SAFETY

- School safety is crucial when one is leading a building. The previous safety plan needs to be reviewed and updated. On opening day for staff, the plan needs to be reviewed, and followed in an active drill procedure. This should be repeated on the students' first day. Evacuations, bomb threats, lockdowns, and severe weather should be a part of this drill procedure.
- The safety plan needs to include similar procedures for the cafeteria, the stadium, and the gymnasium. This plan should include evening events when the facility is filled with spectators.
- Share the plan with the police and fire departments, so that if assistance is needed it is clear to the departments which door to use and what part of the building is in jeopardy. The plans should include a map, and all entrances should be numbered both on the doors themselves and on the maps.

CHAPTER 10 DATA

- Utilizing data and measurement is the only method for making critical changes in teaching practice. Staff members need to be trained on how to read the assessment results. Begin with the department chairs, and provide professional development so they can become coaches within their own departments. Provide additional training to all staff members, so that everyone understands the critical need for data interpretation as it applies to classroom instruction.

- Have departments look at the summative assessments used at the end of units to evaluate student progress. Departments should be using the same assessments for the same classes, even though different teachers may be teaching the content.
- Teachers should be using formative assessments to check on student learning during instruction. Lessons can take an entire different direction if students do not understand the content and are too timid to ask questions. Simple techniques such as thumbs up or down, individual use of whiteboards, and "pair and share" are just a few ways of checking for understanding. The literature has a plethora of ideas on how to implement formative assessments throughout the building.

CHAPTER 11: PROFESSIONAL LEARNING COMMUNITIES

- Professional learning communities are the product of the focus groups that were established at the beginning of the year. It is a natural progression. Initially, literature and research were shared, to develop evidence-based practices to address problems that the staff identified in the building at the beginning of the year.
- Book studies are very common with beginning learning communities. It is hoped that as trust begins to develop within the group, teaching practice and grading can be discussed. A critical friendship will hopefully develop over time, so that peer intervention can help all teachers within the group grow professionally.
- Grading is a natural progression, as the learning community grows closer. Looking at grading practice is important, so that students are not failing due to inconsistent subject practice or because they are missing homework. These are difficult but important topics to tackle with your staff.

CHAPTER 12: ETHICAL DECISION MAKING

- Ethical decision making is the most difficult part of occupying a leadership position. Teachers stop leaders in the hallway and request information. Whatever response is given will become law and be shared among all constituents. Before responding impulsively, tell the teacher that you will get back to him or her with an answer. That time will allow you to contemplate all of the ramifications of whatever decision you render.

- Zero tolerance does not stop inappropriate behavior. It will remove a student, but it does not ensure safety within your building or prevent a repeat offense. It is extremely important that you always err on behalf of the student, as that is why you took the position. Past practice and the severity of the behavior, along with consistency, must be taken into account in the decision-making process. Check board policy and guidelines before making any decision.
- Ethical decision making also affects staff members. Always read the teacher contract to ensure you are following the rules. If you do not follow the contract, the outcome could be long lasting, and the students may suffer in the process.

CHAPTER 13: REFLECTIONS

- Reflection is the last thing an administrator thinks about during the school year. To be an effective leader, you should reflect daily on how the day went, how specific incidents were handled, and what needs to happen the rest of the week.
- Using a matrix or framework to document the day is a good habit to develop. Writing the activities of the day down as they compare to the goals of the building will allow you to determine how much of your day was spent as an instructional leader, versus how much time was spent on inconsequential matters of maintenance and correspondence that could have been handled after the teachers and students had left the building.
- Journaling, keeping a personal blog, or even doing something with voice recognition can influence decision making for the future. Collecting feedback from graduating seniors, teachers, and parents using different instruments can guide you in moving forward for the next school year, and help you evaluate your first year as a secondary administrator.

About the Author

Dr. Kevin A. Gorman has been in education for thirty-five years, sixteen of which have been in a role as principal. He has his bachelor's in education, a master's in curriculum, an educational-specialist degree in administration, and a doctorate in leadership studies.

CPSIA information can be obtained at www.ICGtesting.com
Printed in the USA
BVOW071904070312

284657BV00003B/3/P